"This book is pure gold! Read it a first time to be encouraged, then read it again to soak in and apply its life-changing wisdom. Mike Howerton, one of my all-time favorite young leaders, has hit a home run with *Glorious Mess*!"

h;
/e

"Using the story of Jonah as a ʙ   s
that Jonah's story is our story aɴ   ...ᴇnᴛless grace
is still rescuing people like us today. God calls us to extend the grace we receive to others. We are first objects of God's mercy and get to be agents of that same mercy. Howerton has written a passionate, personal, pastoral, and practical look at how God brings his glory out of our messes through the grace of Jesus."

—Mark Driscoll, founding pastor of Mars Hill Church;
co-founder of Acts 29 Church Planting Network

"Mike Howerton's *Glorious Mess* makes you laugh, then makes you think, and pretty soon leaves you prayerful—in a good way. You'll never see the story of Jonah the same after he unpacks it from his unique and liberating perspective. This is a powerful book that will confront you and lift you at the same time."

—Jud Wilhite, pastor of Central Christian Church, Las Vegas;
author of *Torn* and *Uncensored Grace*

"Mike Howerton invites us to wake up and recognize God's invitation to join him in his work right where we are. *Glorious Mess* is a profoundly gracious, funny, and challenging call for ordinary people to truly risk themselves in service to Jesus. I highly recommend it!"

—Mike Erre, pastor of Mariners Church, Mission Viejo, CA;
author of *The Jesus of Suburbia* and *Why Guys Need God*

"Ever been in a mess? Ever feel like a mess? You're not alone. We all mess up. And this powerful book will show you—in practical terms—how to turn your mess into something magnificent that will glorify God. Truly, Mike Howerton delivers the goods in helping us see the immeasurable love of our grace-giving God. You don't want to miss out on Mike's life-changing message (not to mention great communication style). After reading this book you just might discover that your mess has brought you into a life that is more glorious than you ever imagined possible."

—Les Parrott, PhD, www.LesandLeslie.com;
author of *Real Relationships*

"Through our friendship, I've seen Mike continue to be the one who shows up with the soul-penetrating question followed by an encouraging word. *Glorious Mess* is no exception. Mike's words will resonate with the 'rest of us' who are looking for an authentic experience with God that may not fit in more contemporary formulas—and he does it in language that puts you across the table from him at your favorite coffee shop."

—Ryan Meeks, lead pastor of
EastLake Community Church, Seattle, WA

"Mike is a personal friend, a powerful communicator, and a great pastor. Page after page I hear his voice sharing his story and The Story. I see his heart for Jesus and the gospel. I picture the hope he describes even in the messiness of life. *Glorious Mess* is a fresh take on an ancient story. I encourage you to read his book if you're exploring and studying the book of Jonah or if you simply need help walking in, through, and beyond your own glorious mess."

—Jonathon Alexander, senior pastor of
Northshore Baptist Church, Kirkland, WA

"Mike Howerton is the kind of pastor I want as my pastor, and *Glorious Mess* reflects why. Mike is honest and authentic about the broken places in life but also speaks hope into those places. *Glorious Mess* is a book that restores a weary soul. It points to the hope we have in Jesus that the messy places of our lives, under his Lordship, actually become glorious places of hope and promise."

—Dr. Scott Dudley, senior pastor of
First Presbyterian Church of Bellevue, WA

"*Glorious Mess* is both glorious and messy. With a raw and often hilarious voice, Mike invites us to consider the depths that Christ will reach to grasp our hands amidst the mud and muck of our lives and then points to the dizzying heights we can reach in the loving embrace of our Savior. Finally, Christian writing for those of us who don't normally like Christian writing!"

—Christopher Wilshire, cofounder of Egg Strategy Solutions

GLORIOUS
MESS

GLORIOUS MESS

encountering God's
relentless grace
for imperfect people

mike howerton

BakerBooks

a division of Baker Publishing Group
www.BakerBooks.com

Published by Baker Books
a division of Baker Publishing Group
P.O. Box 6287, Grand Rapids, MI 49516-6287
www.bakerbooks.com

Printed in the United States of America

Library of Congress Cataloging-in-Publication Data
Howerton, Mike, 1970–
    Glorious mess : encountering God's relentless grace for imperfect people / Mike Howerton.
        p.   cm.
    Includes bibliographical references (p.   ).
    ISBN 978-0-0810-1391-1 (pbk.)
    1. Christian life. I. Title.
BV4501.3.H73 2011
248.4—dc23   2011036130

The internet addresses, email addresses, and phone numbers in this book are accurate at the time of publication. They are provided as a resource. Baker Publishing Group does not endorse them or vouch for their content or permanence.

12   13   14   15   16   17   18   7   6   5   4   3   2

Contents

This is a magic book . . .
Not because it will give you hope that you can triumph in all
things,
although there is a bit of that.

This is a magic book . . .
Not because it will assure you that you are
accepted and loved exactly as you are,
although there is a bit of that.

This is a magic book . . .
Mostly because it empowers you with the truth:
Whoever and wherever you are,
God loves you and is calling you into something glorious.
Even in the midst of your mess.
No, wait.
Especially there.

Introduction

I am a pastor.
I work in a church.
I am also a mess.
I went with a buddy to Gold's Gym one time. One time. Everyone there looked like Ahhh-nold. Even the women had muscles and a gap in their front teeth. Each one was bronzed, glistening, cut, and lifting more than I could wrap my mind around. (I understood there would be no math at the gym.) I went over to the pink weights, looked in the mirror, and was startled to realize someone had replaced my biceps with those of a third-grade girl. I didn't belong. This gym was for the Big Dogs. I wasn't even a dog, really. More like toy poodle, which science reveals is predominantly rodent. I never went back, opting instead for an intense workout program that consists of wrestling (on the floor with my kids) and surfing (the internet).

I wonder how many times this experience happens in a church setting. A spiritually interested person decides to go to church. When they get there, they are overwhelmed by the fact that no matter who they look at, they don't measure up. The teaching is from a guy who apparently hasn't wrestled with a single sin issue in his life since he became a follower of Jesus, at age four, when he had to repent of making a frowny face after his folks asked him to clean his room. Everyone seated around them is dressed to the nines, votes with a clear conscience, drives a paid-for Volvo, and has children who smile demurely, probably from homes that look like they're snipped out of

11

Better Homes and Gardens. Better than whose home and garden? Mine, for one.

Who can measure up? The above is an obvious exaggeration, but the view from outside is very one-dimensional, unless we take the pains to change it from the inside.

With three elementary school kids, a dog, multiple sports teams, and dozens of neighborhood friends running through it, my home is continually in a DEFCON 1 state of disarray (identified as the most agitated state of peacetime, prewar chaos). I'm personally bringing the harried, wrinkled look in, praying it catches on. My children are wonderful gifts from God himself, and I wouldn't trade them for anything, but they have rarely nodded demurely. My kids tackle demure kids. It's pretty messy where I live.

The truth is, no matter how it looks, most everyone is a bit of a mess.

When I first moved from California to Washington, I drove a 1979 Suburban. It had no heater. Mostly I think a car is perfect if it gets me from point A to point B, but I am now convinced a heater is also essential. One night that first winter, I walked out from my office late, and the entire truck was iced over. I tried to get in, but the driver's side door was frozen shut. If you're from someplace warm (and sane), take a moment to let that sink in: Frozen. Shut.

So I walked around the car and yanked the passenger's side door open. The frozen handle literally broke off, so the door opened but would not stay closed. This did not improve my mood. I noticed my fingers had become icicles. I was carrying a cup of coffee I had brought to keep my hands warm since my heater wasn't functional, but then I noticed my windshield was iced over, impossible to see through. I poured the coffee onto the windshield to melt the ice, because I didn't have an ice scraper. And I didn't have an ice scraper because I'm from Southern California and hadn't used an ice scraper in a long, long time. Like never. So coffee was my plan.

It was a dumb plan. The whole cup froze instantly on the windshield. The passenger door was yawning wide open. My fingers felt brittle, ready to fall off any moment. I crawled into the driver's seat, fixed the loop of my backpack over the passenger door lock, and drove with one hand holding it closed, with my head out of the open driver's window because the only thing I could see through my windshield was the brown liquid that was supposed to keep my fingers and my belly warm on my cold ride home but instead was frozen solid, like my fingers were and like my face quickly became, except for my eyes, which were bleeding rivers of salty joy down my face and forming tiny icicles off my chin. But hey, I was making progress. A mess but moving toward home. We live life like that. We limp along. We tolerate ourselves. We survive our foibles. We put up with our stupidities, with the messes we make, and we roll our eyes at ourselves, swearing under our breath, wishing we didn't make things quite this messy—personally, relationally, and spiritually messy. I wonder if we aren't missing something profound. I wonder if we don't see that in that moment, in that mess, just there where we're stuck, frustrated, or otherwise not all that impressive—that's where God is free to bring his glory. I wonder if that's exactly where his grace is sufficient.

I don't know where you are in all this—how you view your life, your struggles, your trials, your sin. But let me ask: Do you view your imperfections as a canvas for God's glory?

All throughout the Scriptures, we see examples of God loving imperfect people, forgiving imperfect people, and using imperfect people for great and glorious things. God's love for imperfect people is unrelenting. In fact, the bigger the mess, the more glory God seems to get. And of all the glorious messes in the Bible, few are messier than Jonah.

Everywhere I go, people grab me and say, "Pastor, give me some Jonah! I need more Jonah! I've got a fever, and there's only one cure . . . Jonah!"

Okay, not exactly. And there's probably a reason for that.

The flannel board Sunday school story of Jonah smacks of the incredible, the miraculous, and the supernatural. Because it has been viewed in that light, the book of Jonah is too often dismissed as an ancient fable with little practical value for our lives. I googled the word "Jonah," and the top ten sites were for children's books and academic biblical commentary (well, and Jonah Hill, the actor).

How tragic.

It's tragic because one way or another, Jonah's story is our story. He's a mess, just like us. I'm a Jonah. You are too.

When God calls us, many times we run from the thing we know he is gently prompting us to do. When we run, the storms hit. When the storms hit, we turn back to God. When we turn back to God, we see an absolutely incredible return on our obedience. And even after we've experienced God's grace, we need to be reminded again to share it.

God loves both the reluctant prophet and the repentant people. God has a plan for us, even in the midst of our mess, to showcase his glory.

And God has given us the book of Jonah to learn all about it.

In the five acts of *Glorious Mess,* you will encounter no new evidence that the book of Jonah records fact; no scientific studies proving a grown man can actually utilize the oxygen from giant gills to survive; no bizarre but true tale about a sperm whale that was caught and opened up to reveal a family of four living comfortably inside with their twin hairless cats.

If you believe in a God who spoke all things into existence, who holds the galaxies at his fingertips, who is intimately involved in human affairs, and who is capable of loving even the most stubborn human, then the factuality of this story is a nonissue. I know thoughtful Christians who choose to view Jonah as a potent myth, a fable with a heavenly truth built in. I won't argue that point here (although I believe in the historicity of Jonah), but I know we can agree on this: to an infinite God, commanding a fish and sustaining life for a wayward prophet are no big deal. It's harder for me to cook a package of Top Ramen noodles than it is for an infinite God to perform a miracle.

If you don't believe in that infinite God, Jonah is not the book to convince you. I hope you'll keep reading anyway. Regardless of where you stand on Jonah, it's a powerful story of God meeting mere mortals with feet (and heads) of clay and doing ludicrously beautiful things through their messy lives.

That's good news.

God knew you'd pick up this book. God knows you. He knows what you think about, what drives you nuts, when you obsess about the parts of your body, how your significant other drives you crazy sometimes, how frustrated you get with yourself for not being all that you would like to be. In your mess, God showcases his glory. God also knows the incredible plans he has for you—the empowered and abundant and fruitful life to which he calls you.

We are imperfect. His love is unending. Amen.

Listening to God's Voice

The word vocation comes from the Latin *vocare*, which means "to call." God calls us together into one people fashioned in the image of Christ. . . . A vocation is not the exclusive privilege of monks, priests, religious sisters, or a few heroic lay persons. God calls everyone who is listening; there is no individual or group for whom God's call is reserved. But to be effective, a call must be heard.

Henri Nouwen, *Seeds of Hope*

Vocation does not mean a goal that I pursue. It means a calling that I hear. Before I can tell my life what I want to do with it, I must listen to my life telling me who I am.

Parker Palmer, *Let Your Life Speak*

If you suffer from moral anaemia, take my advice and steer clear of Christianity. If you want to live a life of easy-going self-indulgence, whatever you do, do not become a Christian. But if you want a life of self-discovery, deeply satisfying to the nature God has given you; if you want a life of adventure in which you have the privilege of serving him and your fellow men; if you want a life in which to express something of the overwhelming gratitude you are beginning to feel for him who died for you, then I would urge you to yield your life, without reserve and without delay, to your Lord and Saviour, Jesus Christ.

John Stott, *Authentic Christianity*

1

God Speaks to Us

My dad is a first-class fisherman, the kind of guy who skims *A River Runs through It* for the fly-fishing passages, the type who feels more comfortable rigging a fly rod than sending an email.

Me? Not so much.

This may be due to the fact that when I was in third grade, my dad took my buddy Avery and me to the river to fish. He got me all set up, showed me how to cast, and then handed me a rod. I breathed deep, ready to cast with the fluid artistry of a living poem, imagining that seconds after the hook touched the water, fish would strike like traders at an IPO. What happened set my life on a slightly different trajectory.

I reared back and hurled the pole forward to cast. But the line didn't cast. The hook was caught on something. So I yanked harder toward the water. Still stuck. Without looking, I pulled a third time, as hard as I could, intent on getting the hook into the water where it belonged so large fish could bite like they were destined to do, bringing me the kind of frontiersman-type glory that belonged to me, the kind that would land me on one of those bass boat fishing shows . . . if I could just get the stinking hook into the water.

Nothing doing. I turned around to see what the hook had grabbed. It was my buddy Avery.

My first cast and I landed a sixty-pounder.

Amazingly, I had hooked the tip of his forefinger. It startled him, but before he could remove it, I had yanked again, and then again. So he just stood there, silent, pained, and apparently confused, his forefinger being hoisted in the air for him like a parody of an orator, like the animatronic Abe Lincoln in the Hall of Presidents.

I had hooked him, but he didn't yell. I yelled. My dad came running with pliers to remove the hook, wisely administering calm words and a Band-Aid, helping my friend relax, deftly avoiding litigation. That accident ended our fishing trip early. None of us had caught a fish, but I had literally, at the early age of nine, become a fisher of men.

It's an odd story, and this may sound ridiculous, but honestly sometimes I wonder: Was God trying to get my attention in that moment? I wonder if God is trying to get our attention through all sorts of situations. I wonder if he uses the "just speared my fishing buddy" moment and the "just getting my Starbucks" moment and the "just heading to the office" moment. I wonder if *all moments* are key moments. I wonder if the heave and mess of life itself is the medium God uses to speak to us. I wonder if he uses the mess we're in and the mess we cause to bring his kingdom come.

Life whirls around us in kaleidoscopic fashion, surrounding us with noise, emotion, activity, and frenzy. I talk to people all the time who think God doesn't have a call on their life and who have difficulty listening for him because they believe he won't dial their number, all because of their level of mess. But they're wrong.

What Are We Listening For?

I heard a story about a country farmer who took a trip to Times Square. In the center of the mad pulse of city life, he closed his eyes. Then he opened them, looked down, and picked up a beautiful green-speckled grasshopper, which was chirping softly. "How did you know that was there?" his New York friends inquired. "You need to know what to listen for" was the farmer's reply.

Jesus indicates that those who are his will hear his voice and follow him. He says, "After [the shepherd] has gathered his own flock, he walks ahead of them, and they follow him because they know his voice" (John 10:4).

How would our lives change if we knew what to listen for? What effect would it have if we learned how to listen for his voice in the midst of our dailiness, our everyday work and play? According to the witness of Scripture, God does have a call on our lives, a purpose, a plan, a message, and he does care about our moment-by-moment existence. This is an incredibly exciting prospect! And potentially a frightening one as well.

The book of Jonah begins at God's initiative, with the Lord calling this largely unknown prophet into action:

> The word of the LORD came to Jonah son of Amittai: "Go to the great city of Nineveh and preach against it, because its wickedness has come up before me." (Jon. 1:1–2 NIV)

God called on Jonah to do something. God calls his people to participate in his plans. He is constantly doing this throughout Scripture. We find out in a verse or two how Jonah feels about this particular call to Nineveh, but let's stop right here.

We don't know much of Jonah's biography. The biblical book of 2 Kings offers this passing glance: God had spoken "through his servant Jonah son of Amattai, the prophet from Gath Hepher" (14:25 NIV).

That's it. This is the only background material we get on our prophet. He's known as someone who has heard God speak in the past, his father is named Amattai, and he hails from Gath Hepher, which is a five-mile hike from Nazareth. (Oh, *that* Jonah!) Scripture also refers to Jonah as God's *servant*. Now, a mark of a servant, a character quality that a true servant will have, is willingness to do what the master tells him or her. Obviously we don't use these words "master" and "servant" much in everyday language anymore. In fact, these terms remind us of slavery. The movie *Star Wars* uses these terms in a slightly more positive way, but that was thirty years ago and there haven't been any *real* Star Wars movies since then, right? "Yes, Master Yoda" sounds like something from a fairy tale; it doesn't really connect.

What if we try to recontextualize the word *master*? What if the word referred to one who would love you better than you could ever love yourself? What if the things your Master asked you to do were things your own heart deeply longed for? What if serving your Master meant wild adventure—that you could be part of a story that literally impacted history, eternity, and everything in between?

"Yes, Master" Means Adventure?

We know of people who are willing to do whatever God calls them to do. Mother Teresa comes to mind, as does Billy Graham. You might be this kind of person. If not, you recognize this person. It's your friend with the best stories: "It was almost midnight, and I just felt God prompting me to go to McDonald's and ask the person behind the counter if they had given up on their dreams. So I did. And the guy working there says *yes*, he starts crying, and he accepts Jesus as Lord on the spot. He quits drugs, I help him get into college, he thrives, and he becomes the Prime Minister of Luxembourg, where he introduces the 'Cheese Tax,' now known as the single most important piece of legislation on the planet."

This story is fictional, but you know what I mean. You've heard ones like it (or maybe you haven't, but pretend with me).

My friend Tracy lives her life like this. One night on her drive home, she hears God's prompting: "Go to Ruby's." She thinks, "Great! I love the milkshakes . . . Thanks, Jesus." She makes her way toward the counter and passes a lady sitting by herself. She feels a nudge . . . *Talk to that woman.* So she pauses, takes a deep breath, steps through her comfort zone, and says, "Excuse me, hi, I'm Tracy. I know this sounds crazy, but I feel God wants me to talk to you." The woman promptly bursts into tears. She says, "You're not going to believe this, but I'm a widow, and right now I'm feeling overwhelmed, confused, and lonely. And not five minutes ago I was asking God for someone to talk to." God answered this woman's prayer, and he provided Tracy with a great example of his care (plus a milkshake!). But more than anything else, God gets the glory.

Are you listening for God's voice? Are you open to his promptings? In my life I can be a bit of a selective listener. I tend to need God to hit me over the head. Or at least call me on the telephone.

At my previous church, we had a pastoral care cell phone so that if anyone had an emergency, they could get a live pastor on the horn 24-7. One night I was in charge of the care phone, and just before 3:00 a.m., I got a call. I am a normal human (well, *fairly* normal). Translation: I'm not feeling very pastoral at 3:00 a.m. I gathered through my sleepy end of the conversation that this lady's ex-husband was in a coma, as he'd been for several months, but she was concerned that he was nearing the end and had never accepted Christ as his Savior. Could I please come down, talk to him about Jesus, and pray with him?

I am the *tiniest* bit ashamed to say that I didn't *feel* like going to the hospital. (I felt like pretending this was a fever dream and going back to sleep.) I asked helpful, clarifying questions like, "Let me get this straight—he's not your husband, he's your *ex*-husband?" and "He's been in a coma for months, but you think it's important for me to come to the hospital *now*?" Those were not my best pastoral moments. But I reluctantly sensed that God was in this somehow, so I went to the hospital.

It was just as she had described. I spent ten minutes or so preaching Jesus to him. Describing Christ's love. Walking through God's plan of salvation and the necessary role of Jesus on the cross. I talked about how it's not about the good works we do but about our faith in the good work Christ has done. Through all this the man was absolutely comatose. It felt just like youth ministry. Finally I took his hand. I told him that I was going to pray on his behalf now, and if he wanted to accept Jesus as his Lord and Savior, he could squeeze my hand, or blink his eye, or do whatever he wanted to do to affirm this decision, if that was his desire. Suddenly my hand was in a vice grip. He was blinking hard and moaning a bit and nodding his head *yes, yes* and tears were coming down his face. It absolutely freaked me out. But I've never been more certain of a humble response to the love of Jesus than I was at that response. So I prayed with him. I told him afterward that he could be sure of a couple things: God loved him like crazy, and *all* his sins were completely forgiven. He was clean and free and whole. His ex-wife was laughing and crying and praising Jesus. It truly was a miraculous scene. I asked her to keep me posted on how things progressed with him, and I drove home.

About thirty-five minutes later, as I was climbing back into bed, I got another call from her. She wanted to thank me again for coming down. And she told me that he had just died, passing peacefully into a joy-filled eternity. I began to weep, amazed that God would invite me into that kind of adventure.

You might hear that kind of story and think, *Wow, if only God would call me like that!* He is. He *is* calling each one of us, and he desires for us to hear him and follow him where he leads. God is the one who initiates, and God is the one who is calling. The calls themselves are as unique as the people called. And I am convinced that God is calling us often, speaking to us many times, prompting us to join his story regularly, right in the messy midst of our lives.

God Speaks, but Do We Want to Hear?

Many of us are living contradictions. I've done some empirical probing in my own life and have determined this to be true. We want God to speak to us, but we're petrified he'll call us to something uncomfortable, or difficult, or worse . . . something *uncool*. This is why the very first step in discerning God's call is determining how you're going to respond. When the book of Jonah opens with the words "The word of the LORD came to Jonah" (1:1 NIV), we might be tempted to assume that Jonah would be preemptively obedient, just because of his status as the Lord's servant. But he's a mess, as we'll see, and his obedience is arrived at through a unique undersea journey.

Henri Nouwen writes in *Making All Things New* about the singular focus that Jesus had in his earthly ministry—the focus of obedience:

> Nothing in the Gospels is as impressive as Jesus' single-minded obedience to his Father. From his first recorded words in the Temple, "Did you not know that I must be busy with my Father's affairs?" (Luke 2:49), to his last words on the cross, "Father, into your hands I commit my spirit" (Luke 23:46), Jesus' only concern was to do the will of his Father. He says, "The Son can do nothing by himself; he can only do what he sees the Father doing" (John 5:19). The works Jesus did are the works the Father sent him to do, and the words he spoke are the words the Father gave him. He leaves no doubt about this: "If I am not doing my Father's work, there is no need to believe me . . ." (John 10:37); "My word is not my own; it is the word of the one who sent me" (John 14:24). Jesus is not our Savior simply because of what he said to us or did for us. He is our Savior because what he said and did was said and done in obedience to his Father. That is why St. Paul could say, "As by one man's disobedience many were made sinners, so by one man's obedience many will be made righteous" (Romans 5:19). *Jesus is the obedient one.*[1]

It wasn't always fun, it certainly wasn't always easy, but Jesus knew exactly what his response to God's call would be ahead of time. He would respond with obedience. *Yes, Lord*—this was the answer on his lips before the call ever came. Decide now to walk in sync with your God-forged destiny. That's how Jesus did it: preemptive obedience.

In other words, "No, Lord" is a contradiction in terms, an oxymoron. And many of his own tend to act oxymoronically, fairly often.

This is why things get so messy, so fast. Because our first parents, Adam and Eve, told God "No," all of their children are born with

"No" on their lips and rebellion in their hearts. This is true of all of Adam's sons and Eve's daughters. We are sinners by birth and by choice. Our DNA is made crooked by the acts of our family tree, and we continue to bend and break branches with our choices not to respond to God's voice. It's not supposed to be this messy, but it is. We're born into the mess, and we choose the mess. Some of us have turned mess-wallowing into an Olympic event. We're messy medal-winners. We're *that* good at mess. And we've become champions at using our mess as leverage to ignore God's voice.

But as we'll see, even in the midst of the mess, God's call still sounds forth.

MINING THE MESS: **MAKING IT PERSONAL**

• What are some of the reasons I'm hesitant to believe that God still speaks to us?

• Do I believe God still speaks, or was that just for the ancients?

• Do I want to hear from God? Why or why not?

• What makes me reluctant to hear him?

• What are three of my favorite stories of God speaking in Scripture?

• Is God now silent, or are we just too loud?

• Are there cultures or faith communities who seem to hear God more clearly?

2

The Way God Talks

Well, Preacher Boy," you might say, "I would agree with you except for one thing: I've never heard God's call on my life. I haven't heard him speak. What does God's call sound like anyway?"

All we know about Jonah's call was that the word of the Lord came to him. We aren't told how it came. Was there thunder and a booming voice from the heavens? Did God's call come in a thin, small voice in the darkness? Was Jonah lying on his back in a meadow, staring up at the clouds when they formed into the words "Nineveh! Get going!"? Was there an idea he couldn't shake that haunted him like a splinter in his mind? All we know is he was certain about what God was expecting of him.

One of the consistent ways God talks to us is through Scripture. The Bible has accurately been called his love letter to us, revealing to us his will and his invitation to walk with him, not only in this life but in eternity. The Bible contains God's revelation of his general call for each of our lives.

God's General Call and Specific Call

Every follower of Jesus needs to be aware of a general call for them, as well as God's specific call in their lives. As believers in Christ who were made in the image of God, we share a general call. These general purposes are universal, have been much written about, and include the following: love God, love people, serve the world, care for creation, live in the truth, and share the Good News of God's love revealed in Jesus.

Every specific call will be filtered through this general call. A good church will remind you of God's general call on your life and help you embody this general call with excellence and joy. This is one important reason why your faith journey needs to be lived out in the context of a local church.

But God is a personal God as well, so what about his specific call on each of us? Here are some guidelines to help discern God's specific call for us.

His Call Will Not Go against His Word or His Character

God's call will never involve temptation or evil or selfishness. "Hey Mike, I heard from God and he told me to fall into alcohol dependency." No, he calls you to get free through a program like Celebrate Recovery or Alcoholics Anonymous. Freedom from the captivity of sin is *always* God's plan. "Mike, now that I'm in my late thirties, I know God wants me to play video games in my parents' basement and pop my pimples with a protractor." No, he calls you to get a life. "God wanted me to key that car that is so much nicer than mine so I won't be so covetous." No, he calls you to get some help with anger management. God will never tempt us to sinful action or motivation. If you're wondering about maybe not fulfilling your commitments, betraying your friends, shirking your responsibilities, or otherwise following a selfish, convenient path at the expense of others, rest assured, God is not in it.

"When tempted, no one should say, 'God is tempting me.' For God cannot be tempted by evil, nor does he tempt anyone" (James 1:13 NIV).

His Call Will Involve a Need in the World

What this means is somebody gets loved on. Somebody gets blessed. Somebody gives thanks to God. There will always be a practical manifestation of good as you proceed. If you are trying to figure out if something is God's call on your life, ask these questions: Who would this be helping? What *good* is it?

James puts it this way: "Suppose a brother or a sister is without clothes and daily food. If one of you says to them, 'Go in peace; keep warm and well fed,' but does nothing about their physical needs, what good is it?" (2:15–16 NIV).

Answer: not a whole heckuva lot. God is calling us to meet needs with love. Whatever God calls us to be a part of will line up with this in some way. This is as true for the career we take on as it is for moment-by-moment discernment of God's call on us. Jesus is the most valuable gift we ever offer. But don't forget that Jesus himself met physical needs as an expression of love.

By way of example, adoption and foster parenting seem to be on the radar of many Christian families with whom I interact. There are many reasons for this. Adoption is on God's heart (see Eph. 1:4–5), and we read in James 1:27 that true religion involves caring for the orphan. This includes orphan care under the umbrella of a general call. But I also sense a stirring in the hearts of many parents that reveals a specific call. Spouses are stepping through hesitancy and telling one another, "Babe, I think God is opening my heart for adoption." And spouses are confirming, "Yes, I sense this prompting too!" It is easy to see that this call involves so many needs in the world—for the orphan, certainly, but also for the family, for the parent, for the church, and for greater intercultural connection.

God's Call Will Not Manipulate Others

Spiritual manipulation is real. People have been ripping one another off in the name of God for centuries. Let me tell you where it might show up. Let's say you go on a great weekend retreat with a church group where you've had your eye on a single hottie—and there are many hotties in the midst of churches, ladies and gentlemen, which is just one reason why you should be in church (I'm talking to you, single dude, living in the basement of your parents' house popping pimples with a protractor). Let's say after this member of the opposite sex catches your eye that you go up to her or him and say, "God told me to marry you."

Let me teach you the answer to that statement: "Ha. That's funny. You're smoking something that's probably only legal with a medical card." Because announcing to someone that God told you to marry them is manipulation.

I'm not saying God would never play matchmaker. Just the opposite, in fact. I believe he delights in bringing quality followers of Jesus Christ together for a life of love, for marriage, for beautiful babies, for leadership in your church, for leaving a legacy, and so on. I truly *do* think God plays matchmaker. I actually know friends who have said prematurely to their spouse that God is calling them to marry, and things have worked out for them (after intense therapy). But I don't recommend it because I *don't* believe his call ever manipulates.

So here is an idea: if you feel an attraction for a member of the opposite sex, get to know that person. Actually talk to one another. You might Facebook friend them first, but sooner or later, personal interaction really helps. I know, crazy, right?

Once you get to know that person in a friendship, ask them out! I heard about a guy in my church who took his girl to church on their first date. During the sermon, he flipped open his Bible to Song of Solomon. He started quietly amen-ing. She wondered what he was reading, so he pointed her to the verse that says, "your breasts are like clusters of grapes." Thankfully, she cracked up and liked his quirky sense of humor, and this couple just celebrated their fortieth wedding anniversary. So it worked for that guy. But listen to me closely: Do *not* attempt this today! That's not a model you want to copy. I'm pretty sure it's harassment. You'll get slapped, then sued. Steer clear.

Instead, thoughtfully date with honor. Once you've been courting one another with mutual respect for, say, two years, then ask them to marry you. Once they've said yes and you've gone through an engagement period and have asked your pastor to marry the two of you and pray God's blessing on your life, and the pastor has pronounced you husband and wife, and you've kissed, and you are on your way to the reception in the back of your limo, just the two of you, absolutely in love and committed for the rest of your lives together . . . *then*, for the first time, you may lean in real close and whisper something like, "Since the first time I saw you, I've known this has always been God's plan: for us to be together, for love to unmake and renovate us, for my heart to be shattered and quickened by the gift God has given me in you." Then attack one another in passion. At that point it's a holy grope!

You have to become a quality catch before you can catch quality. But don't use God to manipulate a heart. God's call will never manipulate.

Nor will God's call coerce. My daughter Alex and I were at a wedding, which I helped conduct. I performed a portion of the ceremony, which Alex watched from the back. When my bit was done, I turned it over to the father of the bride, who was also a pastor, and he officiated the vows while I took my seat.

Suddenly I discovered Alex had slipped into the seat next to me, because she carefully took my hand and kissed it. "I love you, sweetheart," I whispered. "I love you too, Daddy," she whispered back. Then I looked back up to watch the ceremony, where the father of the bride was choking up as he recounted his personal joy over his daughter and her choice of a husband.

For the briefest instant I saw myself at my daughter's future wedding (a blubbering mess) and saw my baby girl standing with joyful pride next to her man. In that moment, I prayed silently the same prayer that I've prayed hundreds of times: that God would guide my daughter and protect her; that he would ground her in wisdom, courage, and graceful strength; that he would carry her to that day when she leaves my care and enters the adventure of covenant. And I prayed for that special, God-favored man, that he is growing even now in wisdom tempered by grace, strength tempered by gentleness, and great joy tempered by great responsibility, and most of all, that he would know God and pursue him with all his heart.

I realized as I was praying that my daughter probably didn't know that her mommy and her daddy were praying for the man she would someday wed. So I decided to tell her. "Baby," I leaned down and quietly whispered, "I want you to know that your mommy and I are already praying for the man you're going to marry."

She leaned her head forward and eyed me from over her glasses. Her expression was curiously skeptical and serious, and I could tell that in this matter she didn't trust my judgment.

Deadpan, she asked, "Who *is* it?"

Even at eight, arranged marriages don't land on receptive soil.

Unfortunately, there are a myriad of other ways people have used spirituality to manipulate, coerce, profit, and ultimately destroy. Think Crusades, Inquisition, or Testamints (which are apparently Altoids sanctified, packaged, and sold to combat demonic halitosis). Manipulation happens. As you ascertain the validity of the call you believe God is placing on your life, search your heart for any sinful motivation, any thoughts of power, greed, or pride. If you find it, repent and get humble again before Jesus, because his call won't involve manipulation.

His Call Will Involve the Desire of Your Heart

God made you for a specific purpose. Your unique set of gifts and your unique history have a prominent place in God's plan for humanity.

Frederick Buechner wrote, "The place God calls you to is the place where your deep gladness and the world's deep hunger meet."[2]

God made you for a reason. He wants to use your passion to change your world. He calls you to bring the light and joy of his kingdom with you wherever you go, and this will involve the desires he's given you.

I had the honor of lunching with Gary Haugen, president and CEO of an organization called International Justice Mission, and hearing him share how IJM came into existence. Buechner's quote has proven true in his life. As Haugen wades in and helps bring justice to those struggling under oppression and IJM becomes a voice for those who have no voice (helping slaves be set free, widows gain rights, orphans live without fear, etc.), Haugen knows he's not only meeting a true need in the world, he's living the life he desires to live. This is because Haugen is being true to the way God wired him. And this brings God pleasure!

God's Call Will Require a Step of Faith

"Truly I tell you, if you have faith as small as a mustard seed, you can say to this mountain, 'Move from here to there,' and it will move. Nothing will be impossible for you" (Matt. 17:20 NIV).

Anything is possible with God. Literally anything. More and more I'm seeing belief not as an idea to hold but as a life to be lived. Faith will always involve a step. It will challenge your comfort zone. If you can do something without totally relying upon God's goodness and strength, it probably isn't the fullness of what God is calling you to do. The call God places on your life will be something guaranteed to fail without God's involvement. For years I have stared at a Post-it note on my computer that keeps me aware of the role God plays in fulfilling his call in my life. It says, "I'm so far out on a limb with you now, God, that if you don't show up, I'm toast!"

I hope you see how this changes the definition of success. Suddenly success is primarily about having a bold enough faith to follow God's call, no matter what the outcome. Mother Teresa said, "I do not pray for success, I ask for faithfulness." Of course, we want both! But if that isn't possible, it is important to remember that faithless success isn't success at all. The call of God required Jonah to take a step of faith. He had to have faith that God had spoken, faith that God knew better than Jonah did, and faith that God would provide for the adventure he was sending Jonah on.

God's Call Will Not *Neglect Wise Counsel*

"Plans fail for lack of counsel, but with many advisers they succeed" (Prov. 15:22 NIV).

If you feel a sense of where God is calling you, pitch the idea to friends and family. Talk about your dreams to those who know you well. A small group of believers with whom you share accountability can play the role of a sounding board. Trustworthy friends who share your values and know your history are indispensable! People who love you and who aren't impressed with you can tell you the truth about how they sense God's call in your life. That doesn't necessarily mean they're right. But it often does help in the clarification process. When you process through the thing you believe God is calling you to, you will receive back from them confirmation, conflict, or clarity. Each response is helpful in the process of discernment.

FAQs of God's Call

What if I haven't heard any specific call on my life? Does that mean I'm doing something wrong?

Not necessarily. But you might not be asking the right questions. I encourage you to start by asking questions like these and honestly answering them with God's help:

- How am I wired?
- What do I get passionate about?
- Am I challenging myself right now in my life?
- Am I making a contribution?
- Am I being still enough to hear God's guidance?
- Am I in God's Word?
- Am I spending time with Jesus?
- Is my life free from the bondage of sin?

If the answer to the last question is no, I know right now what God's immediate and specific call is on your life. He wants you free. He wants you to do whatever it takes to embrace the liberation that was provided on the cross of Christ. Remember what Paul writes: "Therefore, dear brothers and sisters, you have no obligation to do what your sinful nature urges you to do" (Rom. 8:12).

I know too many people who muck around in the haze of being near God but never really embracing the new, wonderful, incredible, blessed life that God has for them. We have all lived in the haze from time to time. I know I have. This is the essence of our mess. And the challenge is to invite Jesus into the midst of your mess. Jesus died for your salvation in the afterlife, and you have a place in heaven for all of eternity. But Jesus also died for your freedom *now*. Start there. Get the help that you need. Get counsel that encourages you to walk the road of liberation. There is nothing you can't confess because there is nothing God can't forgive. Build into friendships that support you, and support others on the journey. You'll find that your passion, the clarity of God's call, and the strength for tackling the giants all increase exponentially when your life is honestly pursuing freedom. So don't wait!

Now, is God's call for our lives always going to be big? No. It is not the size of the act but the amount of love in the act that matters. Mother Teresa said, "If you can't feed a hundred people, then feed just one." Even a cup of cold water in the name of Christ merits reward. Often we do not see the immediate result of a small act of faithfulness, yet small acts can yield miraculous benefit.

Should I be content with thinking small? Not a chance. God's call might not always be *big*, but it is likely bigger than you think. God is able to do more than we can imagine. Most of our dreams are infinitely too small. God is able to do all things, and because we are his, so are we. The same power that raised Jesus from the dead dwells within us (see Rom. 8:11)! Think about that for a second. The same power that brought Jesus from dead to alive animates your very soul. Through the power of the Holy Spirit, you are a house of the holy! It is time to let God blow the ceiling off your small dreams.

Regardless of what you think about the size of your dreams, God wants to speak into your life, to walk with you into his best. I'm fairly disciplined with a daily quiet time, and routinely I journal my prayers to God. I started this habit in college, and I've found it consistently helps a guy like me focus on God, on his Word, and on prayer. My synaptic connections tend to fire in all sorts of tangentially urgent ways, making silent, focused prayer difficult. However, lately Jesus has been waking me up in the middle of the night. It's been really amazing. I wake up, perhaps through a violent snort, and suddenly sense the presence of the Lord. I've had incredible times with him just processing things by lifting different scenarios, different problems, different people before him. I've been amazed; until recently I've always slept through the night. But I would trade sleep every night for these incredible tangible moments with Jesus. And it is in these times with him that I sense his unfolding call on my life. I sense his prompting regarding certain things. But mostly I simply enjoy time with him. And I dare to think that he enjoys time with me too.

Lessons on a Riding Mower

Let me close this chapter with a point that pulls together everything I've been trying to say.

Six years ago I fulfilled a lifelong dream and purchased a riding lawn mower. And when I would go out to mow the lawn back then, my two-year-old son, Caleb, would want to ride on my lap. He sat nestled into the crook of my elbow, talking up a blue streak, telling stories that were drowned out by the whirr of the mower. But inevitably, after ten minutes or so, I would notice he had stopped talking and begun yawning. This would be followed by his head nodding forward or lolling backward, and soon he'd be sound asleep. So I'd finish the lawn, steering with one hand, holding my sleeping son with the other, and just praise, praise, praise my heavenly Father for giving this earthly father a golden memory of mowing the lawn.

This happened regularly when Caleb was two.

And three.

And four. You get the picture, and no, he does not have narcolepsy.

The first spring weekend this year with clear skies, it was time to do yard cleanup after the winter storms wreaked their havoc all over my suburban dreams. So I cleared branches away and prepped the mower for the inaugural run of the year. I called over to Caleb, "Hey bud, wanna help me mow?" Now, keep in mind, he turns eight this year. He's, like, big.

"Sure, Dad." And he climbed up on my lap, talking a blue streak. Within a few minutes his stories turned to yawns, his head rested on my shoulder, and he was out.

But this time it really hit me.

In the first place, I was overwhelmed with the sense of love and closeness I felt with my bud. My heart was filled to bursting. I took more than a few extra laps to make the most of the time with my boy. And it hit me that in some respects, God must feel like that with us.

It's hard to believe, I know. But it's true. God delights over us. God's love for us is unlimited. Everlasting. Unconditional. Which means that we don't need to perform for him. Even our sleeping on his lap while he mows the lawn brings him joy. God values closeness; that's why he didn't remain distant but came close in the person of Jesus.

I was also struck by the sense of ultimate unconcern Caleb feels while on my lap on the mower. He is lulled to sleep by the hum of the motor, the strength of his dad, and the peace that pervades from knowing he is exactly where he is supposed to be. I thought to myself that this is what Psalm 23 speaks of: complete peace in the strength of our Shepherd. Or Psalm 46: God as our refuge and fortress. Ultimate unconcern, knowing that God has things handled; God knows how to hold me and get the job done at the same time. This is the very picture of safety and contentment, and it's found in our Father's arms.

Caleb is turning eight soon, and boys don't want to sit on their dads' laps forever. I don't know exactly at what age that happens, but the thought of him as a full-sized teen sitting on my lap (tipping the mower over, most likely) didn't evoke the same kind of emotion. I want him to grow to the fullness of stature and wisdom that God has for him, and I want to cheer him to great heights of godly influence and significant contribution. Heck, at some point I want *him* to mow the lawn. But he's my little boy right now. And I'm not ready to lose these moments. So I was thankful again for the chance, just this once more, to have my son zonk out on my lap.

The very best place to hear God's bidding through the messiness and noise of life is the place of proximity. It's the place of drawing near to him. The place of resting in him. Delight in him, and experience his delight over you. My prayer for you (and for me) is this: I pray that in the heat of planning, of running, of achieving and performing, that you would pause. Hear the Lord calling you to draw close to him. God loves you, and as unbelievable as it is, he wants to be with you. Find some time today to climb up in your Father's arms, let him drive the universe, and just rest. He's a strong dad.

And you never get too big for his lap.

MINING THE MESS: **MAKING IT PERSONAL**

Spend some time on God's lap. Write yourself a letter, addressed to you, as if it's from your heavenly Father. Fill it with loving Scripture that God is speaking over you, his beloved son or daughter. For example, "My child, I promise I will never leave you or forsake you. I have loved you with an everlasting love. How great is my love for you? It's endless. My love for you endures forever. I delight over you. I sing over you. I rejoice in our relationship. I have plans for you that are good, that bring you a hope and a future. My plans for you are to prosper you and not to harm you. I have made you wonderfully. I love being your friend."

Allow God to speak his love over you, and include ways that God is delighted in you.

Write how God is calling out your strengths. Include his invitation to courageous living.

Write out how God identifies the desires he has planted within you.

And make sure it's signed at the bottom, "With all my love, your Father."

3

How to Be an Active Listener

In the next act we'll unpack how Jonah responds when he hears the word of the Lord, but I'll give you a clue: it's not pretty.

I apologize for this, but I need to tell a love story. When my wife, Jodie, and I first started dating, we were head over heels in love. We were high on it, like kids sucking helium and singing Chipmunks tunes. We were giddy. She studied full time at a university an hour and a half away from where I did ministry, so we spent a ton of time on the phone. Prior to cell phone technology, we were anchored to land lines and spent moony, sappy, nauseating hours on the phone. Those conversations would end like this: "You hang up." "No, you hang up." "Okay, we'll both hang up together." Pause. "You didn't hang up." "I couldn't. I just want to stay on the phone with you and fall asleep." "Oh! That is so sweet!" (I know. Seriously. Somebody, somewhere, just threw up a little bit in their mouth. But track with me here.)

Because of my love for Jodie, I counted it an honor to do things for her. One morning, after many late night hours on the phone, I drove down to where she was staying just so I could surprise her with her favorite coffee drink. She was delighted. Surrounded by the gentle aroma of Country Green Apple lotion from Bath and Body Works, she kissed me thanks before heading off to class, and I'm pretty sure I floated home.

If she were to ask me, "Honey, can you drive down to San Diego this afternoon?" I'd have said, *Sure!* "Babe, can you help me and my roommate move into our off-campus apartment?" *Absolutely!* "Darling, can you fetch me the moon before Tuesday?" *On it, babe!* I was so in love that to respond to my love's desire was literally a joy for me.

What if this is how we are designed to respond to God? Sure, dutiful obedience is preferable to disobedience, but what if God is most interested in a full-hearted response of love?

"My heart has heard you say, 'Come and talk with me.' And my heart responds, 'Lord, I am coming'" (Ps. 27:8).

I want to be that in love with Jesus. I want to be the one whose heart responds with this kind of pursuit. I want my heart to be fully open to Jesus. It's not open all the time, because I'm a bit of a mess (have we covered this?). But I do know that the Lord has invited me to come talk with him, to be with him, to walk with him.

When you find your contentment in God, when his desire is your dream, there is *nothing* that cannot be accomplished, no star out of reach, no mountain that cannot be moved because God is God, and you are his, and nothing is impossible with him. But this requires active listening on our part.

Participating with God to Hear His Call

I've found five steps to be helpful when striving to listen actively to God's specific call. The disclaimer is this: while certain scenarios might be more conducive for listening than others, God reserves the right to get your attention any old way he chooses. You could pursue discerning his path for your life for weeks, and on just the afternoon that you quit listening, you'll find yourself driving on the freeway, blasting tunes that couldn't possibly be used by God (Nirvana? Bieber? VeggieTales?), when suddenly he invades and you know his call more clearly than your own name.

Step 1: Get Quiet

With some planning, try to secure child care, time away from the office, a blessing from your spouse, or whatever else is required to be on a personal retreat. This retreat does not have to be longer than twenty-four hours and can be effective even in a half-day form (7:00 a.m. to noon). If you have a friend with a cabin on a lake, this is when you ask if you might borrow it for a day. If you don't have a place to go, you can even plan to take a mini–road trip to a scenic or unfamiliar part of your county and do much of this retreat in a coffee shop where nobody knows you. But the main focus is that you are prioritizing time to be quiet, to get before the Lord, and to really press into his call for you. At home the laundry, the dishes, and the task list are too tempting. At the office, you probably should be working (I'm just saying). You must try to flee the bonds of normalcy in order to quiet your mind.

Step 2: Invite God's Spirit

Begin this exercise with prayer, literally inviting God's Spirit to own the time. Invite him to unstop your ears. Invite him to remove your fears. Invite the Spirit to speak God's heart to yours. The Bible tells us that God's Spirit is our counselor and our comforter. So whether you journal your prayers, pray out loud, or pray quietly inside of your head doesn't matter. What matters is that you invite the Spirit to come and bring both his comfort and his counsel. If there are sins you need to confess, if there is business that you need to do with God, this is the ideal time to step once more knee-deep into his grace.

Step 3: Take a Personal Inventory

You need to understand a bit of how God has wired you. You need to be aware of the strengths he has uniquely built into you. Many resources are available to help you in this process. I would suggest a personality test (like Myers-Briggs), a spiritual gifts test (like Saddleback Church's SHAPE test), and a strengths-clarifying test (like StrengthsFinder).

I was amazed at the results I received from a StrengthsFinder test I recently took; my top strength came back as Maximizer. That means I like to find people, projects, ministries, or institutions that are languishing and help them achieve their potential. When my wife heard this, she laughed out loud. I cannot drive by a dilapidated house without declaring how phenomenal it would be fixed up. I'll even start verbalizing architectural design improvements to maximize the property. The problem is, my actual skill set for maximizing construction projects is nil (and my wife reminds me of this). Nor do we have the assets to pay others to maximize dilapidated buildings (my wife reminds me of this as well). I dream like this with all sorts of things:

old houses, classic cars, the US economy. But I can cast a fairly compelling vision of God's preferred future for our church, which probably means I'm in the right spot in ministry.

Many of us compare our hidden weaknesses to the clear strengths of others. Other times we ask God to give us new strengths or gifts. But the truth is that God has given you all sorts of gifts that you are currently not using, simply because you haven't clearly understood how he's wired you. Take an inventory. Take a look at *all* of the weapons God has stored in your arsenal. Then you'll better understand how he calls you to use them.

Step 4: Identify Your Dreams

"Now all glory to God, who is able, through his mighty power at work within us, to accomplish infinitely more than we might ask or think" (Eph. 3:20).

God can do immeasurably more than all we can ask or imagine. That means it's appropriate to wildly dream about fulfilling your most passionate pursuits. The world's deep need and your deep desire will collide to show you God is whispering, "*Here* . . . here it is . . . here is where I'm calling you." I know that by now in your life, you have placed a filter on what it is okay to dream about and what it isn't; some things are possible, but the really great dreams are impossible, out of reach. Don't buy it! As Henry Ford said, "Whether you think you can or think you can't, you're right."

George Dantzig was a career Stanford math professor who in the 1930s was a grad student at Berkeley. His experience in grad school was the inspiration for Matt Damon's character in the movie *Good Will Hunting*.

At the beginning of a class that Dantzig arrived late for, his professor Jerzy Neyman wrote two examples of famously unsolved statistics problems on the blackboard. When Dantzig hurried in, he assumed that the two problems were part of the assignment and wrote them down. He thought the problems "seemed to be a little harder than usual," but a few days later he handed in completed solutions for the two problems, believing that they were an assignment that was overdue.

Six weeks later, Dantzig was visited by an excited professor Neyman, who told him, "George, you don't know what you've done. You have solved a math problem that even Einstein couldn't solve. You've made history."

Of course, Danzig would later joke with his students, "Do you think I would have answered those questions if I had arrived to class on time? If I would have been told that they were impossible to solve?" (By the way, this is why I'm late everywhere I go.)[3] Because he didn't know that they were "unsolvable," he solved them. The opposite is true with us: we typically think so many things are impossible, off-limits, unattainable. They are not. Nothing is impossible with God (Luke 1:37). We can do all things through God who strengthens us (Phil. 4:13). But we have forgotten how to dream. Without dreams, we wither and shrivel, like California Raisins or an Orange County tan in Seattle. Remember why you're doing this: because you're in love with God, and because he's in love with you. He has wired you in an absolutely unique way in order to display to the world his image and in order to bring him glory. So delight yourself in him, and ask him to reveal the dreams he's planted in your heart. "Take delight in the LORD, and he will give you the desires of your heart" (Ps. 37:4 NIV).

Step 5: Set Your Goals and Submit Them to God

Once you have dreamed your dreams, it is time to put them before God. Put them down on paper. Dreams are little better than wishes if they just swirl around inside your head, but when you've thought them through enough to write them out as goals, now they become legitimate, and plans can be made for their accomplishment. I spend time every year working through an updated goals list for four areas of my life: personal (health, friendship, wholeness), career (in my case these are ministry goals), significance (the legacy I'm building), and savor (goals revolving around family enjoyment). I also identify a loose timeline for each goal; some are ongoing, some I'd like to accomplish in this year, and others I put out ten or even twenty years. One thing that seems to work is to prioritize one or two goals in each area to pursue maniacally. At the end of last year, I celebrated that out of seventy-four goals, I had fulfilled twenty-eight. That's twenty-eight more than would have been fulfilled if I had failed to listen to God. I give him all the glory, because he's the one who stirred my heart toward those goals in the first place. And I'm still charging after the other forty-six!

The old proverb says it best: "Commit your actions to the LORD, and your plans will succeed" (Prov. 16:3).

So write your goals out, and submit them to God. This can be a scary prospect. What if he smashes them? Friend, God knows what is absolutely best for you and for the world. He won't smash your best. He will smash your mediocrity and spur you on to your best. He will smash your lethargy and spur you on to productivity. But you must listen to him as you dream.

Remember how God called Samuel?

> The LORD came and stood there, calling as at the other times, "Samuel! Samuel!" Then Samuel said, "Speak, for your servant is listening." And the LORD said to Samuel: "See, I am about to do something in Israel that will make the ears of everyone who hears about it tingle." (1 Sam. 3:10–11 NIV)

Have you ever prayed Samuel's prayer, "Speak, Lord, for your servant is listening"? Be willing to submit your dreams, your agenda, and even your pride to God. Then watch him exalt you and lift you up to your highest potential. Remember, you were made to love God; you were created for his pleasure.

Setting goals is a huge part of actively listening to God. I'm a believer in making decisions based upon those goals and in planning to accomplish great things in life. However, I want to make sure that I submit any and all plans that I have to Jesus. Listen to James: "What you ought to say is, 'If the Lord wants us to, we will live and do this or that.' Otherwise you are boasting about your own plans, and all such boasting is evil" (James 4:15–16).

What this means is that we prayerfully approach goal setting. Always be ready to release your plans in favor of *his*. The best possible way to accomplish goal setting is to simply ask God on the front end how he'd like you to proceed. He knows the way ahead.

I do most of my writing at a world-class coffee shop on the east side of Seattle. They just installed a roundabout at the intersection outside. I am amazed at how confused drivers are as they approach. There are clear signs marking who has the right-of-way and which lanes are supposed to lead to which road exiting the roundabout. Granted, the signs themselves look like characters written on the Temple of the Forbidden Eye at Disney's Indiana Jones ride. But once you learn how to discern the writing, you'll sail right through like a double-tall vanilla latte sails through a certain pastor who likes to write at world-class coffee shops.

But almost every day I'm there, I see a driver completely ignore the signs and go the wrong way around the roundabout. Each time this happens, I cringe at the near misses. Similarly, some people live their life without consulting God, without ever listening to his direction. Spiritually speaking, they're the ones driving the wrong way on the roundabout. Far better to read the signs, which are crafted for your protection and safe advance. But even when you commit your plans to God, there are times when he still steps in and disrupts. He retains that prerogative.

Never forget the truth that this God who calls you, this God who speaks to you and has plans for you, this God is the same God who is one step ahead of you every step of the way!

God Is One Step Ahead

We see this truth in the story of Peter and Cornelius in the tenth chapter of Acts. Cornelius sees a vision ("Go get a guy named Peter"), and Peter has a dream ("Go to Cornelius"). God is one step ahead of them. He calls them both. The amazing thing is, they obey. Hearts are set free. Eternity is changed. The church is expanded. The kingdom grows. And God is glorified.

Because God is one step ahead, Cornelius, Peter, you, and I can live fearless (free to *risk*) with a bias toward action (free to *move*). These are the most radical, permission-giving truths I know.

Some of you are dismissive of this idea, because *of course* God is one step ahead. He is sovereign; he's large and in charge; he knows everything; he has the infinite past and infinite future in the palm of his hand. And I don't argue that theology. I'm there. But I'd encourage you to bring it down to a practical level. He is near *you*. He loves *you*. Personally. Specifically. He's one step ahead of you, inviting you to step into his plan for your life and your ministry, for your joy and for his glory.

Eleven chapters later in the book of Acts, we see Paul living the same truth, although it is not as clearly spelled out. Jerusalem is in a riot, and Paul finds himself again at the center of the disruption. The mob wants to tear him limb from limb, and the soldiers who arrest him have to float him above the crowd for his own safety (see Acts 21:35); the crowd is *that* incensed for his blood. I confess that I've received more than a few negative emails from folks who didn't like a joke I told, clothes I wore, or the way my face looks like Spicoli from *Fast Times at Ridgemont High*. In twenty years of ministry I've dealt with hundreds of emails, but I've never had even one death threat. Paul is dealing with a mob of death threats in one day. I'd call this a bad day in ministry. I'd take time to hole up and heal up a bit. Lie low for a while. You know, survive.

But no, Paul says to the guards at the top of some stairs, "Wait, wait, put me down. I'd like to address them." They put him down, and what does he say to the riotous mob? Is it a soothing PR moment? Is it a gentle answer turning aside wrath? He tells them his testimony, and he tells them about Jesus! (And they are furious!) How does he do it? Where does he get that kind of courage? Why would he take such a risk? Because Paul is convinced that God is one step ahead of him!

He can live fearless. He is free to *risk*. He can live with a bias toward action. He is free to *move*.

This truth is for us as well. Think about your life for a moment. God is one step ahead of you. Think about your role in your family and your role with your friends. Think about your neighborhood, think about your church, think about your ministry. In all areas God is one step ahead of you. He desires great increase in your impact. He has great things planned for your life. He's one step ahead of you. And he calls you to follow him.

You might push back: It's fine for Peter, for Cornelius, for Paul . . . they're Bible heroes. They're not only *in* the Bible; they *wrote* the Bible. I can't even get people to like my Facebook status update! Going for it feels so much more fearful for me than it did for them.

It might help to run some worst-case scenarios. If you follow the radical call of God and fearlessly follow him, stuff might go wrong. Somebody might get mad. You might lose money (during a fundraiser). You might have an idea that flops. Let me rephrase that: you *will* have an idea that flops.

You might be working in a youth ministry and leave an eighth-grade student behind on a trip in Barstow, California, say at the McDonald's shaped like a train station, and drive on for three hours before anybody realizes he's missing . . . I'm speaking hypothetically, of course. But listen, flops make the best stories! Recently I almost burned my church down for a sermon illustration. We were teaching through the book of James, and I was giving a message on the tongue. I was addressing the Scripture that says the tongue is itself a flame, set on fire by hell. If ever there was a Bible verse that begged to be illustrated by torching something, this is the one. So my creative team came up with the idea of buying a cow tongue from the local butcher, placing it on a cookie sheet, and firing it up with lighter fluid. (Their job was to be creative. My job was to keep my gag reflex down.) When we tried it at the first service, I put just a tiny bit of lighter fluid on it, and the flame lasted for just over a nanosecond. That made for a nice, polite, forgettable illustration. But we were going for *more*. So the creative guys and I talked in between services, and we decided to put a little more lighter fluid on. You probably should just watch it—it's on www.gloriousmess.org.

Not only did I barbeque the tongue and almost commit arson in a highly public fashion, I failed to learn ahead of time how to operate the fire extinguisher! What you can't see in the video is that the first three rows of people got doused with extinguisher foam! What do you do in a situation like that? What I did—with the whole church cracking up, with the first three rows running for cover, with my face beet red from almost burning my church down—was walk calmly up to the pulpit and say, "Let's close in prayer." We found folks new seats, and we kept rolling! Why? Because God is one step ahead! And in this case, he showcased my mess to create an unforgettable illustration.

He's one step ahead, and he calls you to himself. In spite of your mess. In the midst of your mess. For your best and for his glory.

MINING THE MESS: **MAKING IT PERSONAL**

Brainstorm a list of places and times when you could go on a half- or full-day retreat. Talk with the people around you about this possibility. Get creative, get excited, get going!

Create a plan for your retreat and follow as much of it as you feel prompted to, although if you've never done one before, I encourage you to incorporate all five steps mentioned in this chapter into your day. Tailor the retreat to your wiring. The goal is to move through the whole process so that you are ready to boil your dreams down to a few tangible goals that God is calling you to pursue.

You can find resources for identifying your strengths, your shape (i.e., your spiritual gifts), and your personality at the following websites:

www.StrengthsFinder.com
www.saddlebackresources.com
www.myersbriggs.org

4

Barriers to Hearing

My daughter, Alex; my middle son, Caleb; and I were walking Scout, our nine-month-old shelter mutt, one day after school. As we walked the trails near our home, some neighborhood dogs started barking. Scout is a bit skittish (the folks at the shelter guessed that he might have had a rough family life as a pup), so he lowered his ears and slinked as far from the barking as possible. The kids said the dogs seemed to be yelling at Scout.

"It's like the dogs are shouting bad words in dog language," Alex offered.

"Maybe they're saying the *F* word," Caleb said with hushed awe (he was six years old at the time).

"The *F* word is so bad, adults go to jail for saying it," Alex added solemnly (she was eight).

"Do you know what the *F* word is?" I asked my first-grade son.

"Yes."

"Did Alex teach you?"

"Yes."

Instantly Alex looked up at me with both giggliness and fear behind her oh-so-busted azure blue eyes. Her face read: "Passing the baton of knowledge along to my younger siblings really *is* my job . . . I'm just fulfilling my duty."

"What is the *F* word?" I asked Caleb gently.

He whispered like we were in a museum, "*Fub.*"

We walked along in silence, leaves crunching under our feet, but the laughter inside me was bubbling up like a torrent of joy. Innocence truly is a lovely, and fleeting, thing. I cherish it for the gift it is, because yes, someday the pastor's kids will have a grasp of all sorts of colorful language. I thank Jesus for the innocence of my angels. And I pray to God for wisdom to be a good dad. Mostly I pray I don't fub things up.

The truth of the matter is, though, even servants of the Most High God do fub things up. We go rogue. We strike out on our own course. We choose our own blind path.

God is calling you. God is calling me. We only have to open the pages of the Bible to see God calling, God guiding, God leading, God sending. Isaiah is one example of a responsive servant: "Then I heard the voice of the Lord saying, 'Whom shall I send? And who will go for us?' And I said, 'Here am I. Send me!'" (Isa. 6:8 NIV).

Isaiah's response is simple and immediate. "Here am I. Send me!" He was operating out of the posture of obedience. He was willing. Whatever God was calling him to, Isaiah was willing to charge hard after it. Notice he did not ask, "Lord, will this be convenient for me? Will this call come with full medical and dental benefits? Can you guarantee my safety? What are the girls like there? Do I have to wear pants? What if there isn't an espresso stand? Do I bring my own coffeemaker just in case? Will it be in Europe? Should I bring an adapter?" Isaiah simply said yes. He knew the very best possible course was heeding the call of his Designer. His decision had been made ahead of time.

No matter what stage of life we are in, there are all sorts of reasons, rationalizations, and excuses to offer God while we go rogue our own way. Here are a few I've heard (and unfortunately used).

"I'm too young. I'll jump in and follow God's plan for my life when I'm older . . . when I've learned a few things . . . when I've had my fun."

The Bible makes it clear that God isn't concerned with how old you are. God has no minimum age requirements in his job description for a servant. He will supply you with all you need when you are willing to follow him, right now, in spite of any resources you may or may not have and in spite of any skill you may or may not have. God calls children to phenomenal things every day. A child had the guts to offer his sack lunch of bread and fish to Jesus, and Jesus fed the multitude (and there were leftovers!). David was a teenager when he killed Goliath. Joan of Arc was a teen when she led her armies, routing the English. Thomas Jefferson was in elementary school when he penned the Declaration of Independence. (Okay, not really, but it would have driven the point home nicely.) The truth is, God can use you now to make a difference. He is connecting your marvelous craftsmanship with a special mission, designed and fitted for you. His call is for you, messy kid!

"*I'm too old.* I used to be an able-bodied tool in God's tackle box, but now I'm just kind of tired. I've put in my time. I've earned the right to be a spectator. Besides, what could I do?"

When I hear or suspect this posture, I basically go nuts. The kindest grace-givers, the proxy moms and dads and grandmothers and grandfathers, the best children's ministers and the smiliest huggers are all in their beautiful golden years! I call these the wisdom years. Mentor *me*, for heaven's sake! Please, for the love of God's glory, for the sake of his church, for the honor of his call on your life . . . please respond like Isaiah! We have a dear saint at my church, named Mel, who is like a spiritual father to me. He prays for me every Sunday before I speak at our church. I don't know his exact age, but he's so old *Jurassic Park* brought back memories, he has an autographed Bible, and I'm pretty sure he remembers when rainbows only came in black and white. (Just messin', Mel! Yes, sir, we'll add a hymn.) He's got a wealth of knowledge and experience for me to draw from.

Daniel was in his eighties when he refused to stop worshiping God and was thrown in the lions' den. He was cast to the lions because he was a threat. His faithfulness and righteousness and service were threatening to the king's advisors, to the stability of a godless world order. What would Christendom look like if every octogenarian was committed to being a threat to the enemy? That is a picture I'd love to see painted. I'm talking to you, Joan Rivers! It is never too late to be significant! His call is for you, messy grandpop!

"*I'm too busy.* With work and family and recreation, with hobbies and side projects, I'm just flat out too busy. Plus, I need to get caught up on *30 Rock* in order to clear out my TiVo."

This excuse is the one that seems to hit across the spectrum of age demographics and socioeconomic levels. It's the mark of a life without margin, so that the rich work of the gospel of love remains ineffective. Love requires time. With busy schedules that dominate every aspect of our lives, we're too noisy even to hear God's voice. We can barely hear the call, let alone carve the margin into our lives to respond to it. When Jesus told the parable of the great banquet

(see Luke 14:15–24), the excuses that were used to beg out were not
outlandish. "I have to close a real estate deal!" "I have to test drive
the new Oxen 220i!" "I have to watch a Gary Smalley video with my
wife!" But they were excuses.

Certainly, God realizes how much time you have in a day. He made
the day. God knows how many minutes are in it. The problem isn't
with our circumstances, our age, or our bank accounts. There are
limitations for each of us. The real problem is that, unlike Isaiah, we
haven't decided the answer to God's question, "Whom shall I send?"
We haven't decided to say yes, no matter what the mission, no matter
what the cost. We have not decided to take up the cross and follow
him. God's call is for you, messy Twitter addict!

"I'm too comfortable. I like my current circumstances too much.
I'm enjoying myself. Could you pass the cheese dip?"

People don't really say that—no one really admits this is the issue—
but it is foundational to all the other excuses. Comfort zones are a
big deal for us in the West, weaned as we are on convenience. But the
call of God will force us beyond our comfort zones, and that by definition is uncomfortable. We don't like "uncomfortable." We respond
to uncomfortable like cats to rain. Yet the compelling reason for us
to step through our comfort zone is this: That is where *life* is! That is
where God's *call* is! That is where the glory of *God* is! We know that
ultimately, if we stay within our comfort zone, it becomes a prison,
choking out life and health bit by bit. But if we allow God to make us
uncomfortable, we can follow his leading into life and health.

It's like going to the doctor, in some ways. Nobody loves going to
the doctor. Going to the doctor is uncomfortable; it feels unnatural.
Why do we go? We go because it leads to health. It leads to life.

I'm turning forty this year, and so recently I went to the doctor
for my 70,000 mile tune-up. Uncomfortable. The nurse walks in
and says, "Undress." She hands me a paper towel to put on. That's
unnatural. I sit on this table that has a long strip of toilet paper on
it. She lies to me, saying, "The doctor will be with you in a minute."
Dozens of minutes mill about in one long, boring, uncomfortable
procession. Finally, the doctor comes in and he does . . . certain
things to me. Experiments. He has this rubber-tomahawk-to-the-
knee experiment and this cold-stethoscope-to-the-chest test and
the Mike-fill-the-bottle game and some other experiments I won't
go into. I so badly wanted to grab his stethoscope and say, "What
kind of dentist *are* you?" (I'm just kidding. He wasn't a dentist; he

was a real doctor.) And then he responds, "Relax, I learned this in prison." (I'm just kidding. My doctor didn't go to prison. As far as I know.)

The point is: you don't go to the doctor because you're sadistic; you go to the doctor because you realize that by moving through your comfort zone, you find health and life. God leads us through our comfort zone and into deeper levels of life, deeper levels of spiritual health, and greater measures of glory to God.

Not Alone

The other thing to keep in mind when it comes to responding to God's call is that God goes with us. When we say yes to God, we will find out that he provides for those he calls. He calls me. He calls you. And he doesn't bail out on us afterward. He shows up, he provides, and the miraculous happens.

Like Jonah and Isaiah, Jeremiah heard God tell him he was destined to be a prophet. He pushed back against the Lord because he felt he was too young, lacking wisdom and communication skills. These were legitimate circumstances in Jeremiah's life, but he used them as excuses. But God is bigger than our circumstances.

> But the LORD said to me, "Do not say, 'I am too young.' You must go to everyone I send you to and say whatever I command you. Do not be afraid of them, for I am with you and will rescue you," declares the LORD. Then the LORD reached out his hand and touched my mouth and said to me, "Now, I have put my words in your mouth." (Jer. 1:7–9 NIV)

Like we might tend to be, Jeremiah is a bit nervous about what God is calling him to do. God made him to be a prophet. That's big. But notice the reassurance God provides. To paraphrase, God says, "Jeremiah, I know what I'm doing. I'm God. I didn't pick you by accident. I have always known you, and I have intentionally chosen you. I know all the mess, I know everything you have ever done, I know what you've left undone, and I still choose you! I love you and I choose you. Now, say this!" And then he downloads his message from an external hard drive. God believes in Jeremiah, God is present with him, and God provides for him. He does that for us too. God designed you—he is calling you back into his original design for you. God knows you'll come alive inside your call, because he made you for it.

A Little Thing Called "Disruption"

You might be thinking, "But I'm afraid of what the implications might be if I totally jump in. I think it might disrupt the plans I have for my life." Now you're getting to the heart of the problem. "For I know the plans I have for me," declares myself, "plans that are mostly petty, entertainment focused, and primarily self-concerned." The Bible doesn't give us insight into what Jonah's life was like when God's call came. We don't know what goals he had. We don't know what plans he was crafting. All we know is God called him away from those things and toward God's goals, plans, and agenda. It was certainly a disruption.

Divine disruption turns your life over on itself. Upside down. Often our best laid plans are completely undone, especially if we haven't submitted our plans to him in the first place. And this—when we are stripped of our selfish and often small agenda—is when history is made.

God's call frequently contradicts my own plans. From an early age I sensed God might have a plan for me, something that would involve building his kingdom by making a difference in the lives of others. But I wasn't exactly interested in a life with no glory, no MTV fame, no giant check on the eighteenth green. A life serving others didn't sound like it had pizzazz. I had big, big plans of my own! As a young boy, I wanted to play football in the NFL; I wanted glory, stardom, *babes*! I wanted to rap and dance with my teammates like the '85 Chicago Bears. Eventually I realized that the NFL doesn't hire players weighing less than 150 pounds and of modest talent. I wasn't "Refrigerator Perry." Not even close! I wasn't even "Mini-Fridge Mike." More like "Styrofoam Igloo Howerton," and I found it difficult to imagine that on the back of a jersey. Also, it's hard to run in flip-flops. Plus my helmet and hair product did *not* work well together.

My plans for myself are always shortsighted because I am a human being. I can only see so far down the road. I can only plan so well. God's plans will almost always disrupt my meager little plans. But they are for good—for your good, for my good, and for the world's—and they will always be better than the plan you had in mind (except your plan to buy dozens of copies of this book to give as Christmas gifts. That plan is still awesome).

Our Lady of Divine Disruption

When God called young Mary, she submitted even though she *knew* it meant major disruption.

Picture a young girl, maybe in her early teens. Imagine your neighbor, a kid in your church youth group, maybe your own daughter or niece or baby sister. Mary is engaged to be married to the town carpenter. She's a good girl but has no discernible halo. She's young and vulnerable and very much afraid.

All of a sudden she is told by an angel that she is pregnant—the world's holiest EPT test. Pregnancy can be a bit of a shocker whenever it is unplanned. But imagine this girl's response: "I haven't even *kissed* my fiancé! I swear it! I mean, we did drink from the same straw when he bought me a Kosher Jamba Juice at the Passover festival, but how can this be?!"

Mary knew the consequences for being pregnant outside of wedlock were deadly. The law called for her to be stoned, and not in a way Bob Marley would have appreciated. With big rocks aimed at her head. Ending, not quickly, in death. This would be no party. Three little birds did not sing sweet songs by her doorstep. Every little thing was not going to be all right.

The angel shares a few other details as well—like that she is pregnant by a divine intervention and the forthcoming child will be the Savior of the world. How would she explain *that* to her parents? How does *that* conversation go over with your boyfriend? "Don't worry, Joseph. I haven't been unfaithful. It's God's baby."

Can you imagine how this news might disrupt a life? Please, do yourself a favor: when you think about the heroes of faith, don't think they lived in a holy bubble where every twist and turn of the road was a lark. That makes them characters in an animated Disney film, living a zip-a-dee-doo-dah day. These people were heroes of faith only because of their submission to God's call on their life, even when they felt their hearts pounding—or breaking.

Disruption? Mary had it.

And yet . . . when she first held her tiny baby against the cold of a stable night, she must have prayed, "Thank you, God, for this *incredible* disruption!" When she saw her son turn water into wine, she must have looked up to heaven and said, "Thank you, God, for this *miraculous* disruption!" When she saw her boy, her baby, tortured and then nailed up on the cross with thorns on his head and a gash in his

side, she must have sobbed, "O God, why this *horrible* disruption?"
And when she saw her resurrected son, she must have shouted out
again in utter joy and amazement, "Thank you, God, for this glorious, *glorious, GLORIOUS* disruption!"

When we look at Mary's response to the angel's visit, we see why
she is a hero of faith. Not knowing at all how this call would play
out in her life, she chose to follow God:

> "I am the Lord's servant," Mary answered. "May everything you have
> said about me come true." Then the angel left her. (Luke 1:38 NLT)

She said yes. She knew who she was: she was God's servant. And
because she knew who she was, she knew what she was about: she
was about whatever God told her. May it be as *you* have said. No
conditions, no strings. I submit to my God.

The pages of Scripture are filled with this humble submission. Abel,
Enoch, Abraham, Joseph, Moses, Joshua, Caleb, Rahab, Gideon,
David, Peter, Paul . . . the who's who of Bible heroes had two things
in common. They were not perfect. In fact, all of their lives were
filled with mess of one sort or another. Even the disciples experienced
infighting, jockeying for position, perpetually smelling like sushi . . .
mess. But they were responsive to God's call. They submitted to his
disruption. And as such, they all pointed the way ahead to the perfect,
responsive, submissive Son.

A Really Hard (and Good) Prayer

Jesus, our perfect model of submission, shows us how to pray:

> He went away a second time and prayed, "My Father . . . *may your
> will be done*." (Matt. 26:42 NIV, emphasis added)

This is the most powerful prayer you and I could ever pray. It is a
complete and total surrender to being in the hands of the living God.
Our own agendas are set aside, our own imperfections laid at his feet.
It's saying, "In the midst of my mess, in spite of my mess . . . your
will be done. I am your servant."

The most extraordinary thing about Isaiah, Jeremiah, Mary, and
Jesus is their posture of submission to God's will for their lives and
what is accomplished because of their submission.

God called, and they answered.

God is calling you. How you answer will determine how much of God's call you'll receive in the first place. Determining your obedient response ahead of time will open you up to hearing his call more clearly, more often. Your posture of responsiveness will clear away the barriers to hearing.

"Whom shall I send?" God asked, and Isaiah said, "Send me!"

Jeremiah responded to God's call in spite of his youth.

Mary said, "I'm your servant."

Samuel said, "Speak, Lord, for your servant is listening!"

Jesus said, "Your will be done."

Jonah heard God's call clearly when the word of the Lord came to him. Then he said, "Get me outta here!"

What will you say? The phone is ringing! Will you pick it up? How will you answer? Commit now to doing whatever it takes to hear, and to follow, God's call on your life.

MINING THE MESS: **MAKING IT PERSONAL**

My prayer is that by this point you've spent some time actively hearing God's voice over you. You've not only confirmed his love but also worked a bit at dreaming, submitting, and goal setting. I firmly believe that there is no "one size fits all" approach to God's specific call in our lives, so I have no doubt that after a similar "listening" retreat, we all will hear different things.

Take a look at the goals you feel God is stirring you to pursue. They might be things like open a business, start a blog, write a book, marry Elizabeth, plant a church, plant a tree, volunteer in the parking ministry, learn to play an instrument, travel to India, kill my TV, be vulnerable in my friendships, or a million other things. But all godly goal setting will have one thing in common: each and every goal will bring glory and honor to the God who planted it in your heart.

Explore how the goals you feel like you're called by God to pursue would honor and glorify him. Journal about the ways that accomplishing these goals would not only fulfill longing in you but bring God's kingdom into the here and now.

Running from God

Anyone who claims to know all the answers doesn't really know very much.

1 Corinthians 8:2

The sayings of Agur son of Jakeh contain this message.

> I am weary, O God;
>   I am weary and worn out, O God.
> I am too stupid to be human,
>   and I lack common sense.
> I have not mastered human wisdom,
>   nor do I know the Holy One.

Proverbs 30:1–3

I know that nothing good lives in me, that is, in my sinful nature. I want to do what is right, but I can't. I want to do what is good, but I don't. I don't want to do what is wrong, but I do it anyway. But if I do what I don't want to do, I am not really the one doing wrong; it is sin living in me that does it.

I have discovered this principle of life—that when I want to do what is right, I inevitably do what is wrong. I love God's law with all my heart. But there is another power within me that is at war with my mind. This power makes me a slave to the sin that is still within me. Oh, what a miserable person I am! Who will free me from this life that is dominated by sin and death?

Romans 7:18–24

5

Tempted to Run

Any good fisherman (or woman) will tell you that you have to know the fish before you can catch them. Oh, you might get lucky and catch something by random chance. But to be a consistently successful fisherperson, you need to know fish. You have to know their habits, what they like and dislike, what time of day they feed, what they feed on, when they'll be in the rapids in the center of the stream, and when they'll be in the cool shadows on the bank. I'm not a good fisherman (see chapter 1), so I can't help you much here, but a good fisherman could!

Fishermen also talk about lures. Lures are fake. Unreal. A top-notch fisherman can make his own lures, tying together something that looks like the mutant offspring of a lime green grasshopper mated with a red shoelace. They're bits of plastic, string, or glittery rubber, and they are perfect representations of the insects they are designed to imitate. Only they come with a nasty surprise.

Now imagine you're a fish. You're doing what you normally do, looking for the insects you normally eat, at the time of day when you normally eat them, when suddenly you see something that looks delicious. It doesn't merely look *like* one of your favorite insects; it looks *better*. Surgically enhanced pupae. Mosquito larvae on Botox. You notice that there are all sorts of real insects around, but this one looks bigger and brighter; this one will satisfy! So in your fishy little brain you have a choice to make: Do you go for the thing that is real *and* good, or do you bite on the thing that just *looks* real good?

It is an important question. Because if you choose poorly, you find yourself wriggling on some fisherman's hook.

And that's the essential decision Jonah was forced to make when he received God's call. It is the decision each of God's servants must face sooner or later. In Act 1, we considered together how God is calling us, and we talked about what God's call looks like and how we can position ourselves to hear his call on our lives and respond. Now we're going to examine how Jonah bites hard on just such a lure.

Running from God Is Unsatisfying

The very first line of the book of Jonah says the word of the Lord came to Jonah, because it all starts with God's initiative. Now, there was something surrounding Jonah's call, and it's the same thing surrounding you and me when God's call comes to us. We are surrounded by circumstances! Jonah was in the middle of his own circumstances, and he was familiar with the circumstances Nineveh faced. Nineveh was gritty and tough like South Tacoma in summertime. Like the girls hanging out at Hot Topic in the mall. Like the chewing gum stuck on the underside of the library desk. We're talking super-mega-ultra tough. And Israel had been paying tribute to Nineveh for many years; the Ninevites were the oppressors. They were nasty, smelly pagans who smoked inside restaurants, wore baby seal fur, and used lead paint.

And God says, "Go! Their evil has come up against me! They need to change, or we're going to have some words." And Jonah responds with, "No!" You can imagine he says this with a bit of a nasal twang in his whine. "But Gah-awd! They scare me. Jonah no likey."

We don't know what Jonah had cooking at the time. "God, this is a bad time, I run a prophet hotline . . . I've just opened a kosher deli . . . I've just married and my wife and I are expecting a little Hebrew National!" We don't know what Jonah's status was, but I think God had a reason for not revealing Jonah's situation, because that means suddenly we can identify.

"God, you can't possibly have a call on my life . . . I'm just a housewife." "I'm just a businessman." "I'm just a student." "I'm just a software developer." "I'm just a . . . fill in the blank." God knows exactly what your circumstances are right now. And his call is in the

midst of them. His call is not for "when my life slows down a bit." Not
for procrastinating until "I get a bit more put together." God doesn't
work that way. His glory does not wait until our mess is figured out
(*pssst*—it never will be); his glory works *through* our mess. And this
is actually really good news.

The word of the Lord comes to Jonah. He's a servant of the Lord.
And we've talked about how servants respond: obediently. With all
this in mind, here's Jonah's response:

> Jonah immediately tried to run away from the LORD by going to Tarsh-
> ish. He went to Joppa and found a ship going to Tarshish. He paid for
> the trip and went on board. He wanted to go to Tarshish to get away
> from the LORD. (Jon. 1:3 GW)

He bit the lure called escape! God called Jonah, and he ran like a
kid runs from cough syrup. He chose what looked good instead of
what *was* good. He chose "feel good" over "real good."

Many times that is our response as well: we run from God because
we have our own agenda. Perhaps you've felt his stirring. Maybe as
you've actively listened, you've sensed God "calling" you to something:
perhaps to start a church or serve in a ministry, to write a book or to
write your vows and marry your girlfriend. And you might have other,
different plans. When your plans trump God's plans, you're running.
This principle is also true with the "small" elements of God's call. God
calls us to walk daily in humility and obedience to him. To forgive that
grudge. To treat people well even when we're frustrated with them. To
stay close to Jesus. When we put it off, we're running. When we walk
in pride, in disobedience, or even in casual disregard, we're running
from his call for us. We've got circumstances, hopes and dreams for
our lives, and God's call comes crashing into the midst. Whenever we
go our way instead of God's, we're biting the lure.

Now, listen, we don't have to conclude Jonah was going to Tarshish to open a medical marijuana shop. He may have been planning
on starting a Bible study, or preaching God's love, or launching a
ministry to feed the homeless pugs of Spain. We don't have to assume wicked intentions; even so, he was running from what God had
called him to do.

The Bible is very clear that there are two types of sin: sins of com-
mission, where you commit a wrong (you tell a lie, kick a puppy, or
sneak your kid's Halloween candy), and sins of omission, where you

fail to do what is right (you don't help someone in need, don't own a U2 album, or run from the thing God tells you to do).

> If anyone, then, knows the good they ought to do and doesn't do it, it is sin for them. (James 4:17 NIV)

Take a moment and think: Is there something that you need to do? Has God put something on your heart, a person in your life, or a challenge ahead of you that you need to tackle? He will help you, but you need to do what he is calling you to do. If not, you will find yourself running from God.

I know several couples who are struggling in their marriages. There are many challenges in marriage, many difficult issues, and no innocent parties. When times are tough in marriage, the lure is to escape the covenant and run. A ship to Tarshish is never far off. I know several pastors who are having a difficult time where God has called them to serve. When times are tough in "church world," the pull is to abandon the ministry and run. The ship to Tarshish looks like a gleaming vessel ready to embark on a leisurely dinner cruise. I know several brothers and sisters who are walking in sobriety of one sort or another in our Celebrate Recovery ministry. I think they're heroic. But I know they hear a constant siren song in their ears—to abandon their honest and humble progress and to run. It's those darn travel posters of Tarshish that make it look so inviting. In each of these settings, the temptation is to run from God.

What about you? What's God calling you to do? And what's your Tarshish? It could be as simple as the reality that God is calling you to put in a full forty hours at work, but in your heart you know you are goofing off ten of those hours. God may be calling you to connect more with your spouse in the evenings, but in your heart, as you walk to the computer each night, you know that you're avoiding this call. It might have to do with the money you spend, the purity you pursue, or the angry words you use.

It is the dilemma Jonah faced. It is the dilemma we face.

Operation: Futile

Question: How do you run from God, who is omniscient (he's all-knowing; we don't inform him of our situation), omnipotent (he's all-powerful; our problems do not stump him), and omnipresent (he's all-present; he is never absent from our need)? How do you run from that kind of God?

Once, when I was trying to illustrate this point, I found a sequence of interesting photographs. Each picture zoomed in on a tiny portion of the preceding photo. The first photo was a shot of deep space with a composite picture of innumerable stars. The next zoomed in to a small corner of the first photo, from hundreds of galaxies to a small cluster. Next, a tighter focus, from the cluster to a single spiral galaxy. Then it shifted to one arm of the celestial spiral. Then it focused on a star in that arm, which was our sun. Then it zoomed in toward the spheres orbiting the sun. Then it focused on our familiar blue space marble, Earth. Each photo zoomed tighter and tighter. The next one peered down onto one continent. The next into a city. Then on a neighborhood. One house. Then down into a tree in front of the house. Then a leaf on the tree. Then the photo zoomed into the cells of the leaf. The next peeked into the molecules. Then the atoms with protons and electrons in orbit. And again upon the subatomic mystery of inner space, to quarks, ironically ending up looking very much like the first picture of deep space. I thought it was kind of cool in a nerdy, BBC, more-interesting-than-cool sort of way. (I was going to buy that series of photos to show my congregation, but the resource was like eight bucks, and I was like, "Eight bucks?!")

God has this total perspective. Try to comprehend it for a moment. Try to understand how vast God is: seeing from the expansive universe to the infinitely small. Then try to comprehend this: not only does God see *all* of that simultaneously, he sees *all* of that throughout *all of history* simultaneously! It boggles my mind. How would you even begin to run from a God like that? You can't. The Bible tells us so:

> Where can I go from your Spirit?
>   Where can I flee from your presence?
> If I go up to the heavens, you are there;
>   if I make my bed in the depths, you are there.
> If I rise on the wings of the dawn,
>   if I settle on the far side of the sea,
> even there your hand will guide me,
>   your right hand will hold me fast.
> If I say, "Surely the darkness will hide me
>   and the light become night around me,"

even the darkness will not be dark to you;
the night will shine like the day,
for darkness is as light to you. (Ps. 139:7–12 NIV)

It's a bit like the old song by the Police. Every breath you take. Every move you make. Every cake you bake. Every smile you fake. God is watching you.

You can't run from God. Now, you *can* stay away from church. As a pastor, I know it is fairly easy for people to hide from me, although it cracks me up how often I see guilty-looking people out in the community. I'll be at the gym (although if you saw me, you'd know how ironic it is for you to catch me at the gym) or a restaurant (much more likely), and I'll see someone who hasn't been around church for a while. And they look like I just busted them, like I'm God's homeroom teacher taking attendance. "Oh, hey Mike, how are things . . . Listen, I've been really busy . . . I'm kind of not into church right now . . . I'm in a weird . . . oh look, my ride's leaving (*insert fake asthma attack here*). I'd love to stay . . . (*typically more coughing*) . . . gotta go."

Regardless of whether you go to church, running from God is goofy. It just is. We try it all the time, but it's goofy. (I used the thesaurus and found words like *ludicrous* and *inane*, but I'm pretty sure the best word to use is *goofy*.) Goofy like the person next to you on the airplane stealing your pretzels and then pretending nothing happened. Goofy like George Bush Senior trying to freestyle rap. Goofy like Tom Cruise falling in love or me attempting a jump shot. Just some goofy things to help you understand how goofy it is to run from God.

If we learn anything from this man named Jonah, it is that you can't run from God. Or at least you can't run from God forever. So in some ways the question is, how soon will you turn back? Will it take getting fired? Will your spouse have to leave you? Does your son or daughter have to lose all respect for you first? Or would you like to make the decision to follow God's call a little earlier? It's up to you, really. Nobody can make the decision for you.

Keep reading to learn what it took for Jonah:

But the LORD hurled a powerful wind over the sea, causing a violent storm that threatened to break the ship apart. Fearing for their lives, the desperate sailors shouted to their gods for help and threw the cargo overboard to lighten the ship. (Jon. 1:4–5)

Everybody has a god, or more than one. Everybody places their trust somewhere, leveraging their hopes and dreams somewhere. When a crisis hits, that is the first thing they go to—and these sailors are heaving prayers up like grappling hooks: help, help, help! In America we don't have the same kinds of false gods, but we do have them, and we turn to them in crisis. These gods have names: Money. Connections. Prestige. Accomplishments. Possessions. Pleasure. (Note: these false gods are exposed as impotent when unemployment rates rise and economies stumble.)

Where's the prophet of God in the midst of the frantic praying? Comatose. "But all this time Jonah was sound asleep down in the hold" (Jon. 1:5).

As people run from God straight into a life-sized hurricane, they mentally and spiritually are in a deep sleep. We respond with a party, with a substance, with a relationship, with entertainment. Distractions numb our souls to sleep. We choose our own brand of anesthesia.

Notice that it is a pagan captain who wakes Jonah and encourages him to call out to God. Jonah is a prophet of the one true God, and the pagan captain is telling him to pray! God can use anybody or any experience to wake us up:

> The captain went to him and said, "How can you sleep? Get up and call on your god! Maybe he will take notice of us so that we will not perish." Then the sailors said to each other, "Come, let us cast lots to find out who is responsible for this calamity." (Jon. 1:6–7 NIV)

Casting lots is an ancient way of drawing straws, and it implicated Jonah as the guilty party. The dice landed on Jonah as the culprit. Because he was.

MINING THE MESS: **MAKING IT PERSONAL**

• What are some of the reasons people try to run from God?

• Have you ever tried to run from something you knew God was calling you to?

• What was God calling you to?

• Why did you run?

• How did you feel?

• What opportunities were missed because you tried to ignore God's call? How would God's name have been glorified or God's kingdom revealed if you had said yes to God?

• In light of that answer, why do you think we're often tempted to run from God?

6

The Results of Running

My son Caleb has a rubber snake with vibrant colors and believable markings. It's amazingly lifelike. Now, my wife, Jodie, hates snakes on a visceral level, which is exactly why Caleb loves to hide his snake on her driver's seat, or under her pillow, or in her shower. Each time she discovers the snake, it goes like this: one terror-laden, ear-splitting scream, followed by the chasing of our son through the house, then tickling, which eventually evokes more screams, this time more from joy than terror and mostly from Caleb.

But Jodie doesn't need to scream, you might suggest. Even though the snake looks alive, it's not. You're right. And this can also be true of faith, from time to time. It's where we find Jonah:

> "Why has this awful storm come down on us?" they demanded. "Who are you? What is your line of work? What country are you from? What is your nationality?" Jonah answered, "I am a Hebrew, and I worship the Lᴏʀᴅ, the God of heaven, who made the sea and the land." (Jon. 1:8–9)

Jonah gives a completely orthodox answer, paired with an absolutely unorthodox way to worship: by running from God. The rubber snake is Jonah's. It looks real. It sounds legit. But there's no lifeblood. And yet many followers of Jesus are living in this same tension.

When Jesus was on the scene, he touched lepers, gave sight to the blind, and raised the lame to walk. He healed people with all sorts of maladies and even cast demons out.

To be healed, people pursued Jesus. They sought after him, journeyed to him, cried out to him over the noise of the crowd, dug holes through roofs to get to him, or reached out through the mob to touch him. And he would say to them, "Your faith has made you well." They didn't have a stagnant faith. They were active in their faith. They *did* something—their faith in Jesus resulted in action; it propelled them to Jesus; it moved them, literally; and it was their active, living faith in Jesus that healed them.

At the same time there was all this confusion about who Jesus really was. Jesus asked his disciples about it. "Who do people say I am?" "Some say a madman, some say a radical, some say a guru, some say you are Elijah the prophet come back from the dead." But Jesus kept pressing, "Who do *you* say that I am?" And Peter, one of his followers, declared, "You're the Messiah, the anointed son of God" (see Mark 8:27–30).

Peter was the only one who got it. Everyone else had theories. Everyone else toyed with shoddy, half-cooked theology or rumors. In the whole of the Gospels, literally everyone else was confused about the identity of Jesus. Except Peter. And one other notable exception.

Demon Theology

One particular group had absolute clarity. They weren't confused. Not even a little bit. Who? Demons. Turns out, demons have impeccable theology.

They always called him by name. "You are Jesus Christ, the anointed one of God!" "You are the son of God!" (see for example Luke 4:41). Jesus commanded them to hush, but there is no argument: when it comes to theology, demons know the score. And James uses this as a stark reminder that our faith needs to come with some muscle:

> You believe that there is one God. Good! Even the demons believe that—and shudder. (James 2:19 NIV)

Right now, some of us are thinking about our lives. We're thinking that we believe a good game; we can even talk a good game. But its harder, *and* more important, to live a good game. Faith without deeds is useless. Actions prove the rhetoric, do they not?

Brilliant pastor and theologian A. W. Tozer writes, "Millions of professed believers talk as if God were real and act as if He were not. Our actual position is always to be discovered by the way we act, not by the way we talk."[4]

The Bible says, "You foolish person, do you want evidence that faith without deeds is useless?" (James 2:20 NIV).

Ladies, this makes sense, right? If a guy says he loves you, but he never calls; if when you do go out, he makes you pay; if he talks bad about you behind your back to friends; if he pretends not to notice you when you're in public together . . . is it going to matter that he *says* he loves you? Or are his actions going to have to back up his declarations? When it comes to our faith, we need to do better than the demons. Orthodoxy or "right belief" is important. But it must be accompanied by orthopraxy—right living! Jonah says he worships the one true God of the universe while he is actively trying to escape God's call. At this point, you could argue, my son's fake snake is more lifelike than Jonah's faith.

Whenever we run from the Lord's call for our lives, in big or small ways, this is the unusual predicament we find ourselves in. It's not good, but it's not at all hopeless. We simply need to wake up.

Waking Up

Paul, in Ephesians, tries to shake us from our slumber with the words "Wake up, sleeper" (Eph. 5:14 NIV). Jonah is waking up; he is beginning to tell the truth to himself and to his companions. He tells them he's been fooling them with a rubber snake.

> This terrified them and they asked, "What have you done?" (They knew he was running away from the LORD, because he had already told them so.) (Jon. 1:10 NIV)

I love this nonsequential fact that is inserted parenthetically. I have three elementary school aged kids at home, so the only stories I hear told are nonlinear, Tarantino style. The book of Jonah makes me happy like home. How does Jonah respond? Keep reading:

> The storm was getting worse. So they asked Jonah, "What should we do with you to calm the sea?" He told them, "Throw me overboard.

Then the sea will become calm. I know that I'm responsible for this
violent storm." (Jon. 1:11–12 GW)

The first glimmer of hope in this hopeless chapter is that Jonah
recognizes he is responsible for his own actions—and he is responsible
for the consequences that follow those actions. That is a big lesson.
When you and I learn that lesson, we take a giant leap forward on
our spiritual journey.

Instead, the men did their best to row back to land. But they could not,
for the sea grew even wilder than before. (Jon. 1:13 NIV)

Translation: when it comes to our will versus God's will . . . he wins.
Like a grasshopper vs. your windshield at eighty miles an hour.
Like Pierce Brosnan vs. Daniel Craig in a "007"-off.
Like anybody who makes Oprah mad vs. Oprah.
In other words, going toe-to-toe with God carries with it no possible chance of success. God wins. The absolute worst place you can
find yourself is in a rowing competition with God.
Let's personalize what we see in Jonah's life: when we are not right
with God, storms are everywhere. When we run from God, relationships stop working, friendships are shallow, family life is sticky, the
future seems unclear and stormy. Your personal attitude is in a shaky
place, so you have to try to distract yourself and find false substitutes
to make yourself feel better. You are running from God's best. You
don't have peace, but you're lulling your soul to sleep, medicating
your soul with any number of distractions.
I've experienced this. From an early age I knew God wanted to do
something with my life. I knew God was calling me to use my life
to help others understand his love. But the last thing I wanted to do
was listen to God. So I began to run in little ways at first: in my dating relationships, with ego and popularity, and then with partying.
The interesting thing was that I was uncomfortable with myself. As
much as I embraced people and partying and smiles and laughter, it
was all to cover the hurt I was hiding inside. I knew my heart wasn't
right with God. So I was spending all of this time and energy running
from him, trying to build this fun, wonderful life apart from him. I
traveled all around the world looking for peace, but I never found that
destination because everywhere I went, there I was. I was building a
life, but the foundation was a mess, so no matter how hard I tried, I

was always watching things fall apart. This is how it works when we are out of alignment with God.

Theological Chiropractic

When we are out of line with God's will, all other things in life are affected. Have you experienced this? Vertical relationship with God and horizontal relationships with others cannot be mutually exclusive; they affect one another. Think of your spine. When your spine is straight and healthy, your nervous system functions, your muscles work, and mobility is a breeze. Imagine a bizarre pre–Thanksgiving Day accident in which just as you're bending down to retrieve the cranberry sauce can you've dropped, a frozen turkey slides out of the freezer and lands on your head (hey, it could happen), and suddenly the vertebrae in your neck are thrown out of whack. You experience pain in your neck, in your back, and down your arms, and if the situation continues to deteriorate, if your spine continues to break down, the result can be paralysis or chronic pain. Your spine doesn't delight in causing you pain; it is simply how you are wired. When it is vertically healthy, it affects all of your horizontal movements. Your spine is the structure through which the rest of your activities are funneled. (If you get one thing out of this book, I hope it's the importance of spinal integrity.)

Spiritually, your spine is your right vertical relationship with God. One of the roles I play as a pastor is spiritual chiropractor. When believers come together, we have an opportunity to get adjusted. When you humbly approach God through your church, fellowship, or small group, you allow the Lord to adjust you. When this vertical relationship is right, all of the other activities in your life have the freedom to flourish.

That is why I proclaim with joy (and with Paul), "Wake up, sleeper! Cry out to God. God doesn't want your destruction. God wants your attention. The things he has for you are too big to put on hold. Run to him, not away from him, and watch him do things of greatness that you never would have dreamed."

So they cried to the LORD for help: "Please, LORD, don't let us die for taking this man's life. Don't hold us responsible for the death of an innocent man, because you, LORD, do whatever you want." Then they took Jonah and threw him overboard, and the sea became calm. The

men were terrified of the LORD. They offered sacrifices and made vows
to the LORD. (Jon. 1:14–16 GW)

Notice that the sailors ended up worshiping God. This is a part
of how God brings victory out of hopeless scenarios, beauty out of
tragedy. God will receive his glory through your mess one way or
another. Any two-bit idol can bring good things out of good circumstances. It takes the one true God of the universe to bring good out
of the tragic, the disobedient, the rebellious, the messy strata of real
life in a fallen world.

We don't know what happened to those pagan sailors ultimately.
We do know that in that moment they recognized that Jonah's God
was truly the God of heaven who made the sea and the land, creating
storms, calming waves, seeking his own. They were in awe.

Are you in awe? God is not only infinitely knowing, incredibly
powerful, and pervasively present. He is also all-loving. Love is not a
mere character quality of God. Love is God's character. God is love.
Irresistible. Overwhelming. Limitless. His love is described in the
Scriptures as unfailing. Unending. Unconditional.

Why would we run from an awesome, loving God like this?

MINING THE MESS: **MAKING IT PERSONAL**

We are tempted to run from God because we think we can, and because we don't trust that his way truly is best for us, for others, and for his glory. When you worked through your goal-setting exercises in Act 1, you were actively listening to his voice, and you were in a position of trusting him more deeply.

Take a look at the goals you felt him prompting you to pursue. Spend some time imagining the emotional victory of accomplishing these goals for the glory of God. Enjoy the feeling of the victory that comes from being faithful to God's call. Spend some time imagining how friends or family members would get a glimpse of God's glory through your obedience.

Journal a prayer to God about his faithfulness in your life, and commit yourself to being faithful to his call on your life.

7

Hitting the Brakes

Many fears plague us mere mortals when it comes to the Lord's call on our lives.

We have a fear of failure. On the one hand we know God's pretty amazing; on the other hand we know all about that guy staring at us in the mirror, and we're not that impressed. On the one hand we know God can handle an expansive weekly task list (we've read Genesis 1); on the other hand our Christmas lights are still up, in June.

We fear God has tapped the wrong guy or gal for this chore. You might remember when Moses tells God, "You got the wrong guy." Or you might remember Gideon, who tells the Lord, "You got the wrong guy." Or you might remember when Sarah laughs, essentially snorting to God, "You really got the wrong guy. *And* the wrong gal." The point is, he's heard it before. From better people than us. It doesn't seem to faze him.

Sometimes we find it difficult to believe God will call us into something great. Our fear is that God's call will somehow be "less" than what we might hope. There is a key principle here, and the sooner we get our arms around it, the better off the world will be: God doesn't call you because he wants to *steal* your life. He pursues you for his purposes because he wants to *bring* you life!

We fear the confusion inherent in God's call. One of the reasons we run is because we often can't see the way from here to there. We might have the goal, but we don't have the plan, and it scares us. But I believe this is where a vibrant faith brings rich encouragement. This is where the rubber meets the road. If you could see the whole way ahead, you wouldn't need God. But God has given you amazing troubleshooting capacities to help you in your day-to-day life as you follow his call.

So if you're running from his call, this is the perfect moment to hit the brakes and run backward into his will. You don't have to hit bottom before you recalibrate and respond to God's call. And if you do, you'll realize that he is pulling for you, providing tools for your success.

Tools for Running Backward

God has given you all sorts of tools for moving in the direction of his call.

Tool 1: God Is with You

God's Spirit literally resides within you once you've given your life to him. This radical truth means that you're never alone. No matter what you face, you never face it alone. Trust him. Maybe you lack trust that God's plan is good, and that's what's caused you to run. Hit the brakes, and respond with trust.

> Trust in the LORD with all your heart
>   and lean not on your own understanding;
> in all your ways submit to him,
>   and he will make your paths straight. (Prov. 3:5–6 NIV)

I have certainly wrestled with decision making and "leaning on my own understanding," until I realized I had a choice. I could trust myself and my own wisdom, or I could trust God's. I could trust *Rolling Stone*, or I could trust God's written Word. I could trust the culture, or I could trust the Christ. You have to make these decisions as well. But you don't have to make them alone. God is with you.

Tool 2: God Made You

Even your wiring propels you toward his purposes unfolding in your life. If you'll let me wax biological, I'd love to draw attention to the construction of your brain. I know most of us know very little about the brain (perhaps you know of the medulla oblongata, which is what makes the crocodile so cranky), but I want to direct your attention to the reticular activating system, the RAS.

Here is how this part of your brain works: the RAS acts as a filter. It filters out everything you don't need to know, which, it turns out, is quite a lot. We are being bombarded with so much every day, so many images, so many ideas. Even on the edge of your consciousness, your brain is picking up everything that is spoken and every image, from life to TV to internet, as you're driving, as you're walking to class, as you're working with customers. You're picking it all up. So many stimuli are around you that if your brain allowed your conscious mind to focus on everything, you would go crazy. Your subconscious does pick it up, and it spills around in the form of dreams. The RAS is the tool that filters what you focus on and what you discard. This is how God made you—just one more reason to be amazed at God's craftsmanship. You came with some pretty cool factory-installed features.

When you set a goal, you program your RAS. You tell the filter what to focus on. Things that you have never seen before are suddenly right in front of your eyes, because you have opened up the filter. God did that for us.

Have you ever gone to the dealership and test-driven a car? For example, you test-drive the now-defunct Saturn. You are amazed at how well it handles, how good the gas mileage is, and the low-pressure, no-hassle salespersons. (If this is the case, I'd love to sell you my ten-year-old Saturn family wagon and chick magnet—the repellent side of the magnet, that is. It is vehicular poetry on wheels, perma-scented with wet dog and kid crumbs. I'll make you a killer deal.) As you drive away from the dealership, you see a Saturn at the stoplight. You drive by a parking lot, and you notice three of them. You turn onto your street and remark that a few doors down, your neighbor drives a Saturn, and you never realized it. Why are you suddenly seeing Saturns everywhere? You have turned your RAS on. Your brain works that well! God made it like that. In many regards, we are made to see what we are looking for. "Seek and you will find" (Matt. 7:7 NIV) turns out to be as much a promise as it is a command.

I saw an angel one morning not long ago. Maybe it was the conversation the night before, at dinner, that turned my RAS on. My daughter, Alex, was convinced that as she watched the trees swaying in the wind, she saw an angel waving at her, bringing her peace.

Remember the earthquake in Haiti? I'm like many, I'm sure. I watched the news from the aftermath of the earthquake, emotionally wrapped up in it. My brother's family is adopting two children from Haiti, and his wife, Kristen, was there visiting with their eight-month-old baby, Karis, when the quake struck. She was evacuated safely with Karis, but the little boy they're trying to adopt had to remain there, and it breaks my heart.

All of this was on my mind while I went on a run with my dog. I was processing it all with God—the mess of this world and my own self-inflicted mess.

Then I went by Little Bit, a therapeutic riding center. It's a place where tiny kiddos who wrestle with physical or mental challenges get to ride gentle horses as a form of therapy. I saw up ahead on the trail a little girl dressed in pink with a riding helmet covering her blonde hair. She was riding a brown horse and high-fiving her caregivers: six adults who walked next to the horse for the girl's safety, support, and encouragement. As I jogged close to her, she turned and took in Scout and me.

It was like the sunshine came out. Her smile was heavenly. Her face shone with delight, and she raised both her itty-bitty arms above her head, squealing, "Oh . . . wow!" She beamed like Christmas morning. I've never been celebrated so richly in my life.

I smiled big at her and her caregivers. I passed her on the trail. And when I was past, I burst into tears, stifling some weird half-laugh, half-sob, I'm-too-out-of-breath-to-be-emotional-on-this-run kind of heaving noise.

My heart was pierced with joy and beauty and ache, with the sunbreaks of holiness in the midst of a broken, fallen world. All is not well, not now, but even surrounded by heartache, there is much to celebrate. And this little girl was celebrating! A man running with his dog! Oh . . . wow! A chance to ride this beautiful horse! Oh . . . wow! Being surrounded by people who love me! *Oh . . . WOW!* She was an angel. I'm convinced of it.

There are wonders all around us. I truly pray for the eyes to see them. I didn't look back, mostly because I was convinced she was an angel, and I didn't want to be proved wrong. But then I was thinking, maybe there *are* angels all around. The Bible tells us to be kind to strangers, because by doing so we might entertain angels unaware (see Heb. 13:2). Angels bring messages of peace. Messages of hope. Messages of joy. Messages of healing. Messages of help.

Maybe that's what the relief workers in Haiti are. Maybe that's what peacekeepers are. Maybe that's what the girl's caregivers are. Maybe that's what you and I are called to be today. But either way, I pray I've turned your RAS on to the wonder of God's presence right here, right now, in the midst of your mess. It's right here where his glory invades.

The point is, when you define where it is that God is calling you, you begin to turn your RAS on! You set some goals for yourself based on God's call, and all of a sudden you see how very possible they have become. When you face obstacles, suddenly you see solutions right there because you have switched on your RAS. This is God's design! This is God's will we are talking about. And this is one more tool he has given to aid us in accomplishing what it is he calls us to accomplish.

Tool 3: God Fuels Perseverance

I know a guy named Nick Vujicic, who was born in Australia without arms or legs and is now a motivational speaker, inspiring hundreds of thousands every year. When I hung out with Nick, I introduced him to several hundred college students, and they were blown away. His joy and vigor was unforgettable. He was so good that one of the students I debriefed with was envious not only of Nick's steadfast joy but of the unusual situation that called it forth as well. In Nick's life, it is Jesus who fuels his perseverance.

Near where I live, a high school kid named Ike Ditzenberger, who has Down syndrome, joined the football team at Snohomish High School. One Friday the team was down by 35 points in the fourth quarter against Lake Stevens High, and they put Ike in. Because of the camaraderie on the field between both teams, Ike ended up running 50 yards for a touchdown, past a dozen "missed" tackles. The YouTube clip got millions of hits (type in "The Ike Special" to see it), and now it looks like a movie deal is in the works. I love stories of those who persevere.

One time they took the apostle Paul out of the city, threw rocks at his head, left him for dead . . . and he waited until they left, got up, dusted himself off, took some Advil, and went to the next town (see Acts 14:19–20). Great people don't know how to quit. This is one of the tools that God fuels in us: perseverance.

Abraham Lincoln had this kind of tenacity. He lost more than he won. He failed in business in 1831, was defeated when he ran for legislature in 1832, failed in business again and had his assets seized in 1833. Lincoln was elected to the state legislature in 1834 (and again in '36 and '38), but in 1838 he sought to be Speaker of the State Legislature and was defeated. In 1840 he won his fourth term in the Illinois House of Representatives. In 1843 he tried and failed to receive his party's nomination for Congress. He tried again in 1846 and was elected, but after only one term in Congress, his party asked him to step down and not run in 1848. In 1854 he lost a bid for the US Senate. In 1856 he was considered for but did not obtain his party's nomination for the vice presidency. In 1858, perhaps thinking his luck had changed, he ran for a Senate seat and lost once again. But in 1860, only two years later, he ran for the office of President of the United States and was elected not once but twice. That's a pretty dismal record if you're focused on the failures. But it's an incredible story of tenacity and triumph if you're focused on his impact. Because he refused to quit, nobody remembers Lincoln's defeats. Nobody remembers the litany of his disappointments. If you ask any school kid who Abraham Lincoln was, they can tell you he was one of the greatest presidents America has ever had.[5]

People remember the person who keeps on keeping on.

"That is why we never give up. Though our bodies are dying, our spirits are being renewed every day" (2 Cor. 4:16). Some translations say, "We do not lose heart. . . . Inwardly we are being renewed day by day" (NIV).

Everyone fails. But the people who push through know failure isn't final. So often, the pivotal ingredient is simply a matter of hanging on long enough.

Maybe you need to do that in your marriage. Maybe you need to do that with your kids. Maybe you need to do that with your investments, your generosity, your business, your friendships, your battle for purity, your battle against shortcuts, your health. I don't know where you might feel like giving up . . . but ask God for his staying power. He will fuel your perseverance.

I have a buddy named Jason who was in a band called Saved. Since I was a youth pastor in the town they were from, I tried to support his band as much as possible. I remember going to a concert with my wife, Jodie, that was mostly students milling around in the back, trying to figure out how to talk to someone of the opposite sex. Nobody was paying attention to the band. Well, there was that one guy who was totally paying attention, locked in, standing immobile right there in the front of the stage, alone, eating a package of Oreos, but I'm pretty sure he was stoned. Anyway, Jason defined where God was calling him, and he determined that nothing was going to hold him back from following God's call. He took some risks and faced some scary times financially. The band resurfaced as the O. C. Supertones and went on a great run: multiple albums, multiple tours, and multitudes of young men and women who gave their lives to Jesus because a friend brought them to a Supertones concert.

Jason had a blast doing it and began to see that God had more things in store for his life. So he entered full-time ministry and has been seeing God do some incredible things in his circle of influence. God has brought Jason marriage, family, and ministry and has blessed him with a great enthusiasm for the future because he is determined that nothing is going to get in the way of following hard after God.

God opens doors. God closes doors. Sometimes God calls us to kick open some doors that are currently closed. And he provides tools for us to do exactly that: his presence in us, his craftsmanship of us, his perseverance fueling us, and finally, his delight in us.

Tool 4: God Delights in You

You might be thinking, "Mike, that is an unusual point to draw out of this passage on Jonah. A guy runs from a God who is all over him like the CIA and faces a storm that will kill everyone unless he himself goes overboard. So he convinces pagan sailors to heave him seaward, ending his own life in quiet desperation, knowing that he failed at doing the one thing God had called him to do. I don't see God's delight. In fact, I feel like going to bed and staying there for a really, really, really long time."

Jonah thought it was all over, but for God it was just beginning. Jonah was running from God, seeking an end. God was pursuing Jonah, seeking a new beginning, a new heart, a new dream. In other words, God had unrelenting love for this imperfect prophet.

It's his kindness that woos us to repentance. We are told in the Scriptures that God delights over us with singing (see Zeph. 3:17). As a father delights in his dearly loved children, God delights in you. Sometimes it helps me to get my mind around this concept by thinking about how I delight in my own kids. They don't have to do anything to get me to delight in them. I delight in them because they're mine, and I'm theirs.

I was in my home office early one morning, and it was dark and cold, so I had the space heater running. I was laying on my belly in the middle of the floor with my Bible open, journaling my prayers to God, when my son Caleb padded in, jammies on, Justin Bieber haircut all frowsy. He didn't say anything; he just laid down on my back and turned his head so that it nestled against the back of mine. We just rested quietly there together. I remember thinking, "God, nobody ever told me it would be this good." Out of the stillness, Caleb said, "Dad, can I ask you a question?" "Sure, buddy, anything." I was ready for significance, for profundity, for timeless wisdom to be imparted from one generation to the next. "Dad," he said, "did you know lizards can lick their eyeballs?" I thought, "God, nobody ever told me it would be this random."

I delight in my kids. They don't have to do anything to earn my delight. Sometimes I delight in them when they are sleeping. Other times I delight in them *because* they are sleeping! My delight in them doesn't mean I'm always thrilled with their behavior or their choices. But I am filled with love for them because they're my children, gifts to me from God, and I seek to offer them back to God as gifts.

God delights in you. I don't know where you are right now spiritually, but chances are good there are more than a few of us who have been running from God. We've been running from him in our choices, we've been ignoring him in our lifestyle, we've been pursuing things we hope will bring us pleasure, yet we know firsthand that these things don't deliver, that it isn't God's call for us. The world's way leads to pain, and some of us are experiencing pain right now.

Maybe you are not blowing it hard core; maybe you aren't committing sins. But your sins are sins of omission. You know the good, but you haven't been doing it. That's where Jonah was. It's still a stormy place to be.

God delights in us, and he invites us back into his will again and again. God will work through our glorious mess to unveil his glorious plan.

If you are thinking, "Mike, there is no way God can still use me," then rest in this: *you haven't run too far.* There is no "too far." God has great things in store for you! We see Jonah running from God's call, and it's a one-way flight to Nowhereville. It's a road trip down a cul-de-sac. But the story is not over.

Are there areas of your life where you're avoiding God's call? Is there a relationship that needs attention? Is there a habit you need to drop? Is there an area of your character that you've been ignoring, and it annoys you how often God seems to be bringing it to light? You might think you've been clever in running from God, but you've been the opposite of clever. You've been avoiding your best *and* God's glory. Ignoring God is simultaneously self-focused *and* self-disappointing. Compared to God's plans for us, our way is deeply unsatisfying. Meanwhile, Jesus has been pursuing you. You matter to God. His love for you is unrelenting.

Let him love you and lead you.

MINING THE MESS: **MAKING IT PERSONAL**

Tool 1: God is with you.

Spend some time listing ways God has proven himself trustworthy in your life. Write out ways you have experienced God's presence when you found yourself in need of him.

Tool 2: God has made you.

Thank God for the way he has made you. Spend some time writing down the way God has made your mind, the way he has formed your body, the way he has shaped your life. Recognize that how he has made you is integral to what he is calling you to. And give him thanks.

Tool 3: God fuels perseverance.

Journal some ways you've seen him fill you and fuel you with strength to succeed through difficulty. Recognize that with him, you're stronger than you can imagine. Also recognize that perseverance means difficulty (in other words, when it's fun, it isn't perseverance).

Tool 4: God delights in you.

Remember that God loves you. God delights in you. He is excited about who you are; he anticipates the person you are becoming with joy. Spend some time thanking God for how he delights in you and for what he finds delightful in you.

Getting Out
of Your Glorious Mess

I am this day seventy years old, a monument of Divine mercy and goodness, though on a review of my life I find much, very much, for which I ought to be humbled in the dust; my direct and positive sins are innumerable, my negligence in the Lord's work has been great, I have not promoted his cause, nor sought his glory and honour as I ought, notwithstanding all this, I am spared till now, and am still retained in his Work, and I trust I am received into the divine favour through him.

> missionary William Carey, on his seventieth birthday,
> quoted by Timothy George in *Faithful Witness—*
> *The Life and Mission of William Carey*

Our churches are filled with people who outwardly look contented and at peace but inwardly are crying out for someone to love them . . . just as they are—confused, frustrated, often frightened, guilty, and often unable to communicate even within their own families. But the other people in the church look so happy and contented that one seldom has the courage to admit his own deep needs before such a self-sufficient group as the average church meeting appears to be.

> Keith Miller, *The Taste of New Wine*

"There's much you're better not to know," I say, "but know you this. Know Godric's no true hermit but a gadabout within his mind, a lecher in his dreams. Self-seeking he is and peacock proud. A hypocrite. A ravener of alms and dainty too. A slothful, greedy bear. Not worthy to be called a servant of the Lord. . . . All this and worse than this go say of Godric in your book."

> Saint Godric (1065–1170) near the end of his life,
> paraphrased by Frederick Buechner, *Godric*

8

The Anatomy of a Mess

Why do people lie about the size of the fish that they *almost* caught? Not just lie, why do they *notoriously* lie? Traditionally, this is even worse than the "you should have seen my drive off the twelfth tee" lie. In the surfing community, it's the "you should have seen the waves yesterday" lie. Or consider the way our résumés are colored in just the right ways to be *mostly* true.

I think this kind of lie comes from the reality that we are fallen human beings who long to seem more important than we are. It is so engrained that we laugh when we watch the character on *Saturday Night Live*, played brilliantly by Kristen Wigg, who lies continually, making sure her story beats whoever is sharing their real and authentic story.

This is simply part of the broken DNA of a fallen people.

But Jonah's fish story wins. Hands down. I can imagine him at a cocktail party just off the Assyrian plain. His voice has no inflection. He doesn't seek to convince. He doesn't even try. He knows how it sounds. "The fish was big." "How big?" "Pretty big."

Jonah heard God's call. Then he ran from God's call. Straight into a mess of his own making. Thrown overboard and about to meet a monster of the deep.

Making a Mess of Things

I made a list of times I've put myself into messiness. The list is longer than I'm comfortable admitting. Most of these things were so shamefully stupid that I can't believe they actually happened to me, let alone that I was responsible for them.

One story happened in my formative years at Pepperdine University (Pepperdine. Best. School. Ever. Founded by Solomon. Look it up.) when I got busted for stealing a mattress. Stealing sounds so harsh. I prefer the phrase "long-term appropriation of an unused sleeping apparatus." I didn't need the cheap, plastic mattress. My buddy who was living off-campus did, but I was the one with the truck. You can see where this is going. (If your friend told you to jump off a bridge . . . Silly Mike.)

So I drove him on campus on the first day of school, when everyone was moving into the dorms. The scene was one of mass chaos—freshmen weeping, upperclassmen checking out the bumper crop of young ladies. We went to a dorm that was the "supply" dorm for the rest of them, where there was a pile of mattresses. My buddy and I walked in whistling an innocent tune, grabbed a mattress, put it in the bed of my little 3.5-cylinder Nissan, and drove. Of course we were spotted by the fuzz. Not real cops, mind you; rentals. They were called Public Safety; they weren't packing heat, but they did pack other authentic equipment: walkie-talkies, flashlights, doughnuts, handlebar mustaches, and a fondness for the word "negatory."

And they gave high-speed chase, full siren, lights flashing, in their golf cart.

I floored it in my Nissan, going upwards of, oh, 30 mph, when I realized how hopeless it was. I could hear tinny Public Safety sirens from multiple directions. The Pepperdine campus has only two exits, which both have gates and gate guards who have walkie-talkies too. I suddenly saw the absolute folly of our plans.

So I whipped into a parking spot and handed my friend the keys, and we got out of the truck and sat on the ground just as we were surrounded by Public Safety vehicles, helicopter spotlights, a swat team, and a K-9 unit (that's how it felt, anyway), and we had the right to remain silent. Pepperdine is a sleepy campus, so this was high drama. You would have thought the mattress was worth its weight in diamonds.

Busted. No way out. I received more community service hours than it is possible for a human being to fulfill. I still head back on weekends to serve. My kiddos come with me and pick up garbage, doing time with daddy.

God's Unrelenting Love

What are some of the messy situations you've chosen your way into? Where have you landed and realized, "Wow. That was all me. I did this"? Some of them are probably minor, but others may strike a little closer to home.

Well, here is the good news: God didn't give up on me when I stole that mattress, just like he didn't give up on me when I almost burned down the town of Durango, Colorado (it was an *accident!*), or when I did the other knuckleheaded things on my list that are too embarrassing to mention outside of my counselor's office. God did not give up on Jonah, and God will never give up on you.

This is tangible hope for the messy world we live in, and God has settled the final outcome of our lives (more on this in the next chapter), but we do have a role to play. And the role we play depends on our answer to this question: How messy do we want our lives to get?

Obviously there are all sorts of really messy destinations out there. There is the *Pulp Fiction* kind of messy, which tends to be a bit more violent than most of us prefer, thank God.

There is the lying on a bathroom floor in a lukewarm puddle of last night's party, makeup smeared on your face, wearing a skirt soaked in soggy pepperoni pizza, *and you're a dude* kind of messy. Also referred to as "College: The Hard Way" (see Prov. 23:29–35).

There is the hard-hearted Pharisee where everyone else has a problem, but not you—oh no, the world's going to hell in a handbasket, but you're great, you're normal, you've got it all together *except for the fact that your soul is absolutely frozen*—kind of messy.

And then there's the *I've been swallowed whole by a large aquatic animal* kind of messy. Which is where we find Jonah.

The question you have to ask yourself is, How low am I going to go? How far am I going to run? What risks am I willing to endure until I finally surrender and allow God to get me out of my mess? When I let him work, the mess actually becomes the platform for his glory revealed. How long am I going to try to do life on my own before I realize that God can be present and work even in the midst of my mess?

Unpacking My Mess

Here's how it works in my own life. I'm a pastor. But I'm not a Christian because I'm moral. I'm not a Christian because I'm nice. I'm not a Christian because I'm a spiritual giant.

I'm a Christian because I'm a spiritual asthmatic, desperately in need of an anaphylactic hit of grace just to *breathe*.

I've been in ministry for twenty years, and nothing makes me more claustrophobic than the thought that I've got to have it all together, all my ducks waddling in a warm fuzzy row, and yet I find myself faking just that. I desperately want to say, like Paul said, "Follow me as I follow Christ" (see 1 Cor. 11:1). But when I try to position myself in that elevated cloister, my own hypocrisy breaks out like hives, and I find my head spinning for lack of oxygen.

Somebody with a psych degree is analyzing me right now: "This guy's in ministry? He's a pastor? Of a thriving church? He sounds like a mess." What a monumental understatement. I'm a *glorious mess!* (That's what I've been trying to communicate.) If I don't consciously seize my thoughts and hold them captive, there is no limit to my internal depravity. I might not be capable of desperate acts, but that's because I'm a coward, not because I'm good.

In a flash, my god can suddenly be *self*. My wandering thoughts muse about all sorts of ways to worship *self*, digging little synaptic rivers of eager response as I contemplate how greed, lust, and entitlement are worthy suitors of my soul. My vanity knows no limits either. Unchecked, I could spend days marveling at how great I am, how well put together I look, what a blessing I am to others, how far I've come.

And here's the thing: I don't fear you discovering this. I fear you not discovering it.

I fear making peace with the professional, religious mentality that so often accompanies Christianity.

Every minister, every priest, every pastor, every Christian leader, every youth worker, every believer started out with a sincere love of God and a caring heart for people. I know the Pharisees did. Everyone begins standing knee-deep in grace. Where they drifted, I've drifted. I'm Pharisee Mike, degree mounted firmly on my office wall. I consistently try to show others I'm not the mess I know I am.

Jesus understands all of this and pursues me anyway. He chooses to love me anyway. He chose to die for me, knowing how fickle, how ridiculous, how undeserving I so often am. The clearer my view of sin is, the larger my understanding of God.

One of the oldest prayers in Christian tradition (and virtually the only thing I learned in Greek class at seminary) is the breath prayer, "Lord Jesus Christ, Son of the Most High God, have mercy on me, a sinner." I can still say it with a Greek accent (not so much classical Greek or modern Greek but three-shots-of-ouzo Greek): "Kyrie Yeay-su Christo, Elay-eh-son may, a-mart-alone." Sound it out. Go on. You've just uttered a two-thousand-year-old prayer, the same prayer some of the first disciples of Jesus uttered. The ancients remembered intensely what Pharisee Mike forgets. Recognizing our mutual need of God's unbelievable grace is what allows God to use our glorious mess for his glorious kingdom! His love for imperfect people is unending.

In my college days my mess looked like licentious Belushi from *Animal House*. These days my mess looks like the legalistic prison warden from *Shawshank Redemption*.

When these temptations of mess come knocking on the door to my heart, requesting an audience with my soul, Lord Jesus Christ, please nail them to your cross. Again. And again. I find that the only rest there is, the only peace I know, comes from a confessing dependence upon God's mercy.

No Mess Here

Caveat: For those who are not in any sort of mess right now, remember these wise words as you look upon the messes of the masses: "There but for the grace of God go I." You and I are always very capable of making a few dumb decisions that land us in the belly of the beast.

Paul wrote to his Corinthian brothers and sisters of the faith, "So, if you think you are standing firm, be careful that you don't fall!" (1 Cor. 10:12 NIV).

Regardless of whether we are in the midst of mess, we can experience an essential lesson from Jonah: the first thing to do is embrace the truth that God is all we need.

MINING THE MESS: **MAKING IT PERSONAL**

Take a messy inventory: make a list of messes that you've unwisely opted into over the course of your life. The purpose of this exercise is not so you can brag to your friends about how wonderfully bad you are but rather to get you in the mind-set of knowing God's grace, which is larger than we can ever comprehend. Your list could include selfish behavior, addictive cycles, or simply conversations that you entered into blindly and saw explode in misunderstanding and pain.

Categories for your personal reflection:

1. Relational messes. Situations that got messy with friends, dating relationships, teammates, or work colleagues. Unpack your role in each situation, and explore the consequences of the mess.
2. Family messes. Pray through situations with parents, siblings, kids, and (where appropriate) your spouse. Nobody knows how to put the thumb on the bruise like family.
3. Stupidity messes. Although this could pertain to all categories, this refers to any self-destructive activity, from substance abuse to reckless behavior.
4. Spiritual messes. This may be philosophical ideas you've embraced that have led to inaccurate worldviews or errant theology you've held that's led to judgment, condemnation, or spiritual arrogance.

The more specific you make your inventory, the more thorough your confession before the Lord. Remember that your clarity over sin gives you a clearer picture of Christ's grace. After you complete your list, go through each item and confess it to Jesus. Invite his grace to enter in and cover it. If some of these are ongoing issues, bring them before a trusted friend for prayer, counsel, and encouragement. Never forget that his grace is sufficient for you.

9

Two Ways Out

God provides two ways for us to get out of our mess. Hint: one way is more painful than the other.

Listen to how God took Jonah out of his mess:

> Now the LORD had arranged for a great fish to swallow Jonah. And Jonah was inside the fish for three days and three nights. (Jon. 1:17)

I love this word "arranged." It reminds me of making a reservation at a restaurant, as if God spoke to some angelic host in charge of the sea: "One giant blue whale at 2:00 p.m. near Jonah's boat, please."

Then we read that Jonah was alive inside a fish for three days? This is hard for us to get our minds around, granted. This is not a common occurrence. There is a reason we don't read this story on CNN weekly. Things don't typically stay alive inside of other things that have eaten them. Tapeworms do, but that's just gross. Again, going back to a God perspective: Which is it harder to do, to create life or to sustain life? People sustain life every day on every continent. Thirty-three Chilean miners were rescued after spending two months underground, their lives sustained and restored to them. Physicians in all lands have figured out how to keep people alive, even when circumstances are against them. So I'm comfortable believing that God could pull this off.

The deeper question is: Is God's miraculous power to save available for us today? And emphatically I'm arguing yes, *yes*, *YES!* Trusting in this God, through Jesus Christ, is what opens us up for the full grace and life he had in mind for us from the beginning.

Can you mentally picture Jonah's situation? He is absolutely immobile. He's stuck in pitch blackness. More significantly to us, I imagine Jonah was confronted with his aloneness and dying on the inside, feeling like a failure, riddled with shame.

Somewhere in his isolation, Jonah realized that there was nowhere left to turn. He had no options left. All of the things he had relied upon in the past were gone! Cleverness, relationships, good looks, prophet-popularity, his privilege as a Hebrew, his prejudice against Nineveh, his designer robes, his convertible sports camel—none of that mattered. The mirage of winning apart from God disappeared. He embraced the truth: "The only thing I have is God." And with this humility it hits him: "God is all I need."

> From inside the fish Jonah prayed to the LORD his God. (Jon. 2:1 NIV)

When my daughter, Alex, was born, she was immediately taken from us and placed in the neonatal intensive care unit. We visited a little while later, and she was wired up in a clear plastic incubator box. We weren't allowed to hold her. We couldn't feed her. This was our first child, and we went home without her, an empty car seat in the trunk. This was *not* our plan. And one day, when I drove back to the hospital to visit her, I stepped off the elevator, looked out a plate glass window, and lost it. I wept like I've never wept in my life. All my frustration and all my helplessness and all my love for my daughter, everything just came out. And I realized that God was all I had. Sometimes the only way God can give us peace is when we come to the end of ourselves and simply give up.

Godliness is perfecting the art of the early surrender.

But Then One Day . . .

We don't like change. We will place ourselves in perilous situations again and again simply because it is how we've done it in the past. The experience provides a certain amount of comfort, so we'll stay in a physical relationship, or we'll continue to flirt with the same temptations, because change is tough. We realize our actions aren't the best, but they fall within the realm of what's known.

What's known has brought us some small benefits in the past; that is why we continue the same patterns of behavior. There is some kind of payoff. But typically we know we're heading toward bankruptcy. And sooner or later, we've got to pay the piper.

We find ourselves running from God, content with our own agenda, trying to satisfy a spiritual void with material things, pleasure, relationships, or substances. Until the pain of our current situation becomes greater than the pain of change, we continue in our self-defeating ways.

Let's say you have a term paper (or tax filing) due. You put off the pain of the paper until the pain of not doing it outweighs the pain of doing it (like at midnight before its due date). You change your actions because what you associate pain with has changed: the potential failing grade became more painful than the thought of actually doing the research, so you chin up and write it.

The same principle is true in much more serious situations. People fail to end adulterous relationships because they perceive the pain of doing so to be worse than the pain of continuing the relationship. But then one day the husband gets a phone call from his wife, and she tells him, "I want you and your things out of the house by 3:00. I know about Debra." People who initially "borrow" a few hundred dollars from the company, perhaps to pay a few bills, keep embezzling thousands upon thousands because they think the pain of stopping is worse than the pain of continuing. But then one day the police show up, and the pain shifts.

Jonah kept running and running because the pain of doing what God told him to do seemed worse than the pain of running. But then one day he ended up in the belly of the beast.

The Other Way

God knows there is no greater wake-up call than the alarm clock of pain, but he wants to keep us from these "but then one day . . ." moments. And yet he won't spare us from them if we insist on continuing our flight from him. He loves us too much to allow us the perpetual wounding of ourselves. The thing you need to know is that God has given us the ability to choose change before things get so painful. You don't have to be in pain right now to choose God's way. You simply need to experience an understanding of this truth: your way, my way, and the world's way eventually lead to pain. I've been there. You have too. We can choose to forego the pain and walk with God.

In the midst of his pain, Jonah prays:

> I called to the LORD in my distress,
>   and he answered me.
> From the depths of my watery grave I cried for help,
>   and you heard my cry.
> You threw me into the deep, into the depths of the sea,
>   and water surrounded me.
>   All the whitecaps on your waves have swept over me.
> Then I thought,
>   "I have been banished from your sight.
>   Will I ever see your holy temple again?"
> Water surrounded me, threatening my life.
>   The deep sea covered me completely.
>   Seaweed was wrapped around my head.
> I sank to the foot of the mountains.
>   I sank to the bottom,
>   where bars held me forever.
>   But you brought me back from the pit, O LORD, my God.
>   (Jon. 2:2–6 GW)

The last phrase in another translation says, "But you, O LORD my God, snatched me from the jaws of death!" (v. 6 NLT). Jonah faced the jaws of death on one hand and literal jaws on the other, and they snapped on him as the unlikely agents of God's love. Jonah's prayer to God essentially says, "I'm dead without you, but your grace is sufficient."

Which is true for us as well.

MINING THE MESS: **MAKING IT PERSONAL**

Warning: Humility required.

Think of an area of your life that might be out of alignment with God's best. Consider:

1. Attitude: What outlooks are you currently holding that are faithless or selfish?
2. Behavior: Where are your actions revealing a distance between your life and God's call?
3. Thought Process: Do you have patterns of thought that sabotage your relationship with Jesus or with others?

I imagine that while one or two areas may come to mind immediately, there are probably other areas that are insidiously hidden, perhaps behind theology, self-confidence, or some other concept that is good in itself but can be a mask for some brokenness that we hold. Be humble enough to ask God to search you. Ask him to reveal anything within you that is causing you to run from him into a mess. When you come up with areas of your life that need to be brought to God, journal the answers to these questions:

1. What is it going to take for me to leave this area behind?
2. When is the pain of necessity going to be greater than my fear of change?

10

Improving Your Life by Changing Your Mind

I grew up in Southern California, where it never rains. Three hundred fifty-five days a year you suffer through sunshine. But the other ten days, the sky splits open and water falls with reckless abandon. Whenever that happened, my brother and I would partake in the pinnacle of kid-dom: mud football.

One year, after a particularly wicked deluge, my brother and I grabbed the Watkins twins and headed down to La Tierra Elementary School, which had a grass gully, perfect for our particular needs that day. Fields were closed all over town, but we went down to the gully, which had two inches of standing water. We had a blast! Every tackle would send you sliding for yards and yards. The ball was like a greased pig, which meant tons of fumbles and gang tackles and laughter.

I remember tackling one of the Watkins twins (I think it was Craig, might have been Chris; I could never tell them apart) and watching him skim across the surface of the water for something like four miles and thinking, "I might be in heaven!" When he got up I noticed something stuck to his shoulder. I peered closer, wondering, "What *is* that?" Now, there was a huge, concrete sewage runoff drain right next to the gully. And apparently during heavy rains, all sorts of things got backed up, and I don't know if the apartment complex immediately next to the school burst a pipe or what, but I do know we didn't really pay attention to the flotsam in the gully until I noticed that something on Craig's shoulder. I peered closer and suddenly realized it was a soaking wet piece of toilet paper. In that same instant I realized that the smell surrounding me was a bit more pungent than a typical mud football game ought to smell. I yelled out, "We're playing in POOP WATER!" and we bolted for home as fast as we could. My mom saw us running up the front walkway and locked the door. "You're not coming in this house like that!" So we hosed off in the front yard, trying to get the nooks and crannies and ears and mouth contamination-free.

Talk about an instant mental transformation. One minute I thought I was in heaven. Next minute I was in hell.

Sometimes in life we need our thinking to be transformed. Sometimes we think we're having fun until we realize we're rolling around in sewage.

When I was not walking with God in college, I used to find certain things and behaviors alluring. God has transformed my thinking enough that some of those things are no longer attractive to me. This isn't true for all of these temptations (how I wish it was), and that's a part of the journey that I'm on. I've talked to our Celebrate Recovery pastor about this, because his story is similar to mine. Sometimes God changes our thinking instantly, yet more often it is a process of obedience and struggle. This is where our faith journey becomes about walking with God day in and day out. One of my favorite quotes is, "The tough thing about life is *it's just so daily*."

Magic and Holiness

Last month I took a study trip to Israel. On my first morning in Galilee, I woke up early, jet-lagged, and turned on the television. This was regular television, mind you, not cable, not some pay-per-view channel—just regular TV. Instantly I saw a topless woman staring back at me. (To be honest, I actually don't remember if she was staring, but parts of her body seemed to be.) I quickly turned the channel to Anderson Cooper and started my travel workout routine of push-ups and sit-ups. I'd be lying if I said I didn't want to turn the channel back. But I didn't do that. I worked out to CNN, turned the television off, went downstairs to breakfast, and told my travel buddies about it.

Porn felt out of place on the beautiful shores of Galilee, where Jesus taught and healed and joked with his disciples. For that matter, so did Anderson Cooper. I realized I felt let down. I felt let down by me, because the temptation to lust was even here, and I always feel I should be above that temptation, but I am not. I also felt let down by an illusion shattered. I had been holding the illusion that this would be a magic trip with holiness spilling all around, magically infusing me through my feet, as it were, as I walked the footsteps of Jesus.

But holiness isn't magic. Holiness is hard work. It's a choice to make the same decision that Jesus made when he was tempted. It's a choice to lean into God's Word. It's a choice to draw near to God the Father. And it's a choice to allow him to transform your thinking.

Transformed Thinking

On my own, I will tank it. My life management skills are hopelessly wanting. Left to my own devices, it's the gutter for sure. Running from God is a ticket to Nowhereville (which I've learned is actually in New Jersey). God's way is lovingly, graciously, amazingly the best way.

Returning to God may seem like it requires some sort of sick, humiliating obstacle course that God makes us run before getting back to him, but that's really not the case. Returning to God requires a humble recognition of where running gets us. You come to the place where you say, "I don't want to continue to waste my time and my life. The pain of continuing in sin has eclipsed the pain of change. I understand that my answers are found in the person of God, through Jesus Christ."

This transformation will change our behavior. It will change our perspective. And it will change our thinking, including the value we place on certain things. God wants to transform our minds. Paul wrote pastorally to the church in Rome,

> Don't copy the behavior and customs of this world, but let God transform you into a new person by changing the way you think. Then you will learn to know God's will for you, which is good and pleasing and perfect. (Rom. 12:2)

Notice the progression. Reject the death-dealing patterns of the culture around you and let God change you by changing your thinking.

Then you will see God's will for you, which is "good and pleasing and perfect" (Rom. 12:2). Those three words, "good and pleasing and perfect," can end up sounding like, well, Bible study words, but what Paul is saying is, "Listen, if you take your focus off of what this world offers and place it on what God offers, get ready for rewards beyond your wildest dreams—a life of meaning and deep joy."

Jonah's Transformation

Jonah finally remembered the Lord. He hit rock bottom and stopped running:

> When my life was ebbing away,
>   I remembered you, LORD,
> and my prayer rose to you,
>   to your holy temple.
> Those who cling to worthless idols
>   turn away from God's love for them. (Jon. 2:7–8 NIV)

Jonah had idols. An idol is anything other than God that we bow to, anything that we rely on, anything that we cling to. In the ancient world, there was a whole pantheon of false gods. People would carve statues of wood or stone and pray to them for fertile lands, smooth seas, cooperative camels, and winning lottery tickets. Clearly we see in these first chapters that Jonah had at least two.

The idol of "my way is best," which is called self-sufficiency.

The idol of "my prejudice," which is called self-superiority.

Jonah knew God. Jonah knew all about him, and he loved him and worshiped him. He was the guy at the church service with arms raised, hollering praise and holy, but he still had idols. He had traveled far with them, and they had served him well. You may know God. You may know all about him. You might love him and worship him, but you might still have some idols in the closet that you bring out when you slip back into the old mentality. What are your idols? What is it that you cling to instead of God?

Jonah tells us what to expect when we try to keep our idols: we forfeit grace. When we cling to known, safe, comfortable, and impotent false gods, we miss out on the grace God has showered on us through Jesus. Idols turn us from God's love. We miss out on the "graced" life that he invites us into, a life we enjoy living, a life we feel grateful to share with others. We see that Jonah has changed. He is done with that idolatrous thinking, at least for now. He says:

> But I, with shouts of grateful praise,
>   will sacrifice to you.
> What I have vowed I will make good.
> I will say, "Salvation comes from the LORD." (Jon. 2:9 NIV)

In spite of all that had happened to him, or maybe because of it, Jonah was in a place to be thankful to God. He understood that salvation would come from God, that the only source of salvation is God. God has provided the means of salvation for the entire world, for every man and woman ever born, through his Son Jesus Christ. But God is the only one who provides it. Whatever the adventure *with* God brings will be infinitely better than the plans Jonah had *without* him.

Jonah experiences transformation. He does an about-face. He changes his mind. He decides to no longer run from God but to call out to the God who called him in the first place. He rejects the idols that he has clung to in order to keep God at arm's length. And he embraces the Lord who loves him in the messy middle.

This is what happens after the hurricane, when we come out of our cellars and begin to rebuild our lives. This is what it looks like to emerge, after years of living in the darkness of selfishness, blinking and unsure into the sunlight of God's love. This is what it looks like to live in bondage for long, frustrating seasons and then to finally begin to embrace your freedom. This is what it looks like to realize that you've been content with complaining and you're ready to live gratefully. It's what happens when you look at all of your friendships and discover how shallow and self-serving these acquaintances are, and you decide to embrace vulnerability so that you might possibly have one authentic friend.

During my last year of college, Jesus embraced me. I had been running from him for years, doing whatever I felt like doing as a halfhearted Jim Morrison disciple, until I woke up late on a Sunday afternoon sick with my sin. My soul was filthy. What festered was the whisper that I had lived here before, that I had always lived here, that this sickness wasn't passing, that it was unto death. I felt hopeless. Life was hopeless. I was weary with the knowledge that I could not change my life. I was haunted by this: if I could have changed, I would have changed already. Instead, I floundered in a mire of my own creating. I took a walk on Little Dume, near where I lived in Malibu, with my dog. The beach was deserted, the sky spit rain; it was November. I remember looking out at the kelp forest swaying in the bay. It looked so peaceful, so appealing. The chaos and guilt and paranoia that was my life longed for the gentle sleep that the water promised. "Swim out, swim down," the siren song played. "We'll hold you, we'll help you." I was honestly in spiritual and psychological pain, and in this moment of my life without hope or future, these were the voices that urged my destruction. I was in the belly of the beast, at the end of the road I had chosen to travel. There was nobody else to blame.

Instead, I looked up. I could see the raindrops falling from a great height. I spoke out loud to the sky, to the God who turned out to be nearer than myself, and I said, "If you are real, and if you want me, then now would be a good time to tell me." It was a prayer heaved skyward from the edge of a cliff. And that was when Jesus embraced me with his relentless love.

Externally, nothing happened but the fall of rain. Internally, Jesus held me. Deep inside, it was his whisper I heard, it was his love that told me, "I have been waiting so long for you." All an observer would have seen was a weeping man standing looking up at the rain. All I saw was Jesus. All I felt was him, providing hope in my hopelessness. Where guilt had been tyrant, his grace brought freedom. Where I saw no future, his future for me was good. I didn't know exactly how laying down my idols of self-sufficiency, control, and pleasure would impact my life. I certainly didn't become perfect in that moment. But the entire trajectory of my life was changed, for the better.

The next day, one of my roommates barged into my room. I was strumming a praise song, I had my Bible dusted off and opened and my journal out, and the smell of stale beer was being replaced by the spring clean of God's Spirit. My roommate stared at me in silence for a moment. Then he said, "What the hell happened to you?"

Grace happened. God gave me what I needed most. He still does.

Jonah experienced this as well. He thankfully trusted that God gives what we need most.

MINING THE MESS: **MAKING IT PERSONAL**

- Do some analysis of the issue of "stinking thinking" in your life.

- Where are you guilty of it?

- Where does your thinking need to be transformed?

- Where are your perspectives routinely dark, selfish, lustful, or greedy?

- Where is there unforgiveness or judgment?

- Where in your life do your behaviors need to be transformed?

- What do you think Romans 12:2 has to say to you?

- In your life, how might you let God transform you? How can you allow God to do his work?

- Clinging to idols leads us to forfeit grace. But rejecting idols opens us up to it. Where are the idols in your life? What are the modern names of those false gods?

- Are you ready to let God transform how you think of them?

11

Rescue Is a Many-Splendored Thing

Jonah needed rescue. So do we.

Everyone has a story of needing rescue. Some of you have stories of your head stuck in between the slats of your stairway banister, or when you got stuck climbing over a chain-link fence, or that frosty winter you got your tongue stuck to a frozen flagpole because some kid named Ralphie triple-dog-dared you. If no one had rescued you, you'd still be there today.

I read about a rescue worker named Steve, awakened at night to help search for a girl who had been separated from her parents during a hike. Steve was instructed to meet a policeman at the nearby home of the girl's family, where they would break into the house to obtain clothes and pictures to aid the search; then he was to head up the mountain to join the search team.

The fun of legally breaking into houses is one of the oft-overlooked benefits of rescue work. So he broke in through a window, grabbed some clothes and a framed photo, and headed to the mountains.

The search scene was chaotic, with a large volunteer force. Everyone wanted to see the photo Steve got, of this beautiful young girl hugging her golden retriever, and it was eagerly passed from hand to hand. Finally the photo was passed to the girl's father. He stared blearily at the photo for almost a minute, tilting it this way and that to get a better view. Suddenly he yelled, "This isn't my child . . . we don't even have a dog!"

Steve's eyes went wide. "*Oh no!*" he was thinking. "We broke into the *wrong house!*" Mortified, he thought, "I've screwed up the search, and I'm guilty of breaking, entering, *and* theft." Quietly Steve tried to become invisible. Fortunately the sensible mom took a look, and the entire crew erupted in laughter. She had purchased that frame the week before and had yet to replace the original stock photo with one of their own family. It all turned out well; the little girl was found almost instantly, and Steve didn't go to jail. (The golden retriever, however, was never found.)

Rescue. Every single one of us longs for it at one point or another.

When the earthquake hit Haiti in 2010, we were all rocked with the heartrending stories of rescue. My wife and I were glued to CNN. We read a ton of rescue stories and saw thousands of images of devastation. One photo particularly grabbed our hearts: a little boy exultant, arms raised high, as several workers hoist him to safety.

In all of the rescue stories we heard, we never once read about someone who was angry about being rescued. We never once heard of someone asking to be placed back underneath the rubble. In a catastrophe, people are aware of their need for rescue. Yet we continually live in the catastrophic reality of a fallen world. This might be why rescue is such a central theme of God's love for us. God knows our deepest needs.

The entire Bible tells a story of *rescue*. Listen to God:

> I'll set up my residence in your neighborhood; I won't avoid or shun you; I'll stroll through your streets. I'll be your God; you'll be my people. I am GOD, your personal God who rescued you from Egypt so that you would no longer be slaves to the Egyptians. I ripped off the harness of your slavery so that you can move about freely. (Lev. 26:11–13 Message)

Following are some additional key passages on rescue:

> Whenever the LORD raised up a judge over Israel, he was with that judge and rescued the people from their enemies throughout the judge's lifetime. For the LORD took pity on his people, who were burdened by oppression and suffering. (Judges 2:18)

> To you they cried and were rescued;
>   in you they trusted and were not put to shame. (Ps. 22:5 ESV)

And he did rescue us from mortal danger, and he will rescue us again. We have placed our confidence in him, and he will continue to rescue us. (2 Cor. 1:10)

Scripture refers to rescue in one form or another over five hundred times. All sorts of people in the Bible were rescued by God: Abraham, Lot, Joseph, Moses, the nation of Israel, King David. It just keeps going on and on. Our God is a rescuing God. When Christ was to be born, Joseph was instructed to give him the name Jesus, which means *he will save his people from their sins* (see Matt. 1:21). He saves from trouble, from enemies, from sin, and he saves us from ourselves!

God Rescues the Undeserving (i.e., Me)

The other day I saw a great question kicking around on Facebook (and yes, I'd friend you), a quote from Andy Stanley:

Are you trying to pray your way out of a situation you behaved your way into?

Oh, Andy! The answer is almost always *yes*! At least in my life it is.

When I was in junior high I had a pyromaniac buddy named Carson (or he had a pyromaniac buddy named Mike). He was spending the night, and he asked if I had ever lit deodorant on fire. I was like: *Of course. Who hasn't? Seriously. We're not in grade school.* And he said, "Not the spray kind"—he was asking about the stick kind. Oh, well, no. I hadn't. Never even occurred to me. So, at 3:00 a.m., we grabbed my dad's Old Spice stick, put it on the desk in my room, and lit it on fire. Suddenly we were staring at a three-foot green flame; it was beautiful, the most glory this junior high pyro had ever known. We marveled at its magnificence, our faces bathed with the glow of Old Spice and joy.

Then I noticed the ceiling above the flame was turning brown and beginning to smolder. I also saw that the deodorant was melting and spilling all over my desk as liquid flame. We panicked and tried to blow it out. Immediately we realized how ridiculous this plan was and promptly descended into stifled laughter. *Stifled* laughter, because obviously we didn't want to wake my parents up as we burned their house down. Fortunately, we grabbed our sleeping bags and smothered the fire out, and then we spent the next three hours cleaning and airing out my room, throwing burned sleeping bags away, and so on. If anyone ever needed to be rescued from his own choices, it was me.

We all need rescuing, even from situations we have behaved our way into. Jesus understands our choices for self-destruction, for stupidity, for choosing evil over good. He sees how we choose sin over purity, our way over his way. He loves us anyway, and he wants for us to experience his rescue. He teaches those who follow him to pray:

> And don't let us yield to temptation,
>   but rescue us from the evil one. (Matt. 6:13)

Here Jesus uses the same metaphor of rescue, but he uses it just a little differently; the rescue Jesus talks about is not only from demons, hunger, or physical disease (although his ministry included these forms of rescue). Jesus loved us so much, he wanted to glorify God by rescuing us from the evil one and the sin he tempts us with, which has separated us from God. Our Savior rescues.

The Rescue of Salvation

I gave this quiz to my congregation. I said, "We're in church, so be honest. How many of you, over the course of your life, have ever, in thought, word, or deed, blown it? How many of you have done something you shouldn't have or not done something you should have? How many of you are willing to publicly admit you've sinned at some point in your life? Show of hands." Virtually all hands were raised. When I asked how many had blown it in just the last seven days, even more hands went up, which doesn't even make sense. Then I said, "If you didn't put your hand up, you're either asleep (I understand . . . I've listened to my sermons) or you're lying, which, last time we checked, was still a sin. That puts us at 100 percent. Simply an empirical observation that supports the Scriptures."

Here is my point: we all need rescue. The Bible tells us,

> God looks down from heaven
>   on the entire human race;
> he looks to see if anyone is truly wise,
>   if anyone seeks God.
> But no, all have turned away;
> all have become corrupt.

> No one does good,
>> not a single one! (Ps. 53:2–3)

In Romans we hear,

> For the wages of sin is death, but the free gift of God is eternal life through Christ Jesus our Lord. (Rom. 6:23)

The wage, or the consequence, or the result of sin is death; just as the effect of an earthquake is being buried in devastation. But then there are these two words: *free gift*! The gift God offers is eternal life in Christ Jesus. God's rescue is under way!

And the way he did that was the cross. The full work of the cross was accomplished when Jesus died a death that he didn't deserve, but you did. Our rebellion made us enemies of God; the wage of our sin earned us the punishment of death. We deserved the cross; because of our sin, we were buried in the rubble of our sin, our brokenness, our choices. But in love God unleashed a divine rescue attempt:

> Jesus gave his life for our sins, just as God our Father planned, in order to rescue us from this evil world in which we live. (Gal. 1:4)

When we realize that we're the ones trapped, that Jesus comes to rescue us, suddenly we recognize it as the most important thing in the universe: the cross, Christ's resurrection; Jesus taking all of our sin and shame and guilt and burden on himself on the cross, paying that price, receiving the wage we deserve for our sin, and then rising again from the dead, proving he was who he claimed to be, God with skin on. Jesus is alive by the incredible power of God, showing us how we might be alive by the power of God as well. What if we viewed the miracle of the cross as the greatest rescue mission the universe has ever known?

God is like the bold firefighter who scales rung upon rung of a giant ladder as the skyscraper becomes an inferno. He bursts through a windowpane, shattering it into a million pieces, thoughtless for his own safety. He feels the heat, crouches down, and crawls to the person who is trapped under a bit of collapsed ceiling, in need of rescue. That person is you. "I'm here," he says. "You're going to be okay." He removes the rubble pinning you down, heaves you onto his shoulder, deftly descends the ladder, places you on solid ground, and gives you a drink of water. God is in the rescuing business.

Now, rewind that scene for a moment. What if when God said, "I'm here. You're going to be okay," you said back to him, "I'm fine, thanks. It's a bit hot in here just now, but I'll get used to it presently." And yet that's what happens when we cling to idols; that's what happens when we run from God. We miss out on his rescue.

The Rescue of Sanctification

Now here's the kicker: God doesn't rescue us just once. We don't get just one "Get Out of Jail Free" card, and once we spend it, it's gone, and if we ever need rescue again, tough. The reason this can be confusing is because of the theological words we use to describe what is happening in the spiritual realms. We *are* saved, once, for all time, for eternal life, and the word used to describe that work is *salvation*. But we *are being* saved, again and again, yearly, weekly, daily, and that work is called *sanctification*. We are rescued from ourselves a multitude of times. We are being saved continually so that we might become like Jesus himself.

An analogy for sanctification in my life is my son Caleb's soccer team, which I've coached for four years. When we began, the boys were placed, as soccer players, on my team. They had uniforms, goals, a ball, and a field. The problem was that they didn't play anything similar to the sport most of the world recognizes as soccer. They played air guitar. They dueled lightsabers. They roared as dinosaurs. One of our boys threw himself into the goal again and again, each time yelling "Score!" People at church who knew I was coaching the team would say, "Isn't it fun how the boys just follow the ball all together in a cluster?" And I'd respond, "It would be glorious if they followed the ball in a cluster! At least then they'd be somewhat interested in soccer!"

Now, in reality, even though they were only sort of knowledgeable and vaguely interested in the sport, they were all instantly soccer players on my team. But over the ensuing four years, they've actually learned the game, they've gelled as a team, and they recently have enjoyed undefeated seasons (you've probably seen them on ESPN). Salvation happens when God places you on his team. Suddenly you've got the uniform and you're on the field. But inevitably you kick the ball the wrong way. You play out of bounds. You might keep throwing yourself into the goal. Okay, not ideal. But God keeps rescuing you, untangling you. He keeps coaching you, and he will continue to rescue you, pick you up, dust you off, guide you, and love you until he can see the character of Jesus revealed in you.

The Rescue of Adoption

I can't even write about adoption without getting emotional, because adoption is the road that God has called my wife and me to walk. We're so excited that this year we've completed the journey, adopting a five-year-old-boy from South Africa named Duzi. He is a miracle. He brings such joy into our home and is a clarion call of God's love to us.

Let me tell you the story of another little boy. Last summer, my friend Josh and I visited this orphanage called iThemba Letu, and we got a chance to see this precious child get picked up by his forever family and say good-bye to all his buddies. He stayed in the rental car, holding hands with his new brother, while all the other children from the orphanage came out and gave him hugs in the backseat of the car. He didn't want to get out of the car because he was so excited about being with his new family. Now, one of the practices of iThemba Letu is that they'll ask the adoptive parents to send a photo album over with some pictures of the life that the child is going to be entering into. They ask for photos of family members, pets, car, house, and school to all be placed in an album. This album is then given to the child exactly ten days before the parents arrive.

The director told us that when this little boy received his album, he wouldn't put it down. He kept walking around with it; he'd sleep with it; he'd keep it with him at playtime; he barely put it aside even for bathtime. He just kept holding it tight, then he'd open it again and again, look at it, and show it repeatedly to everyone at the orphanage, exclaiming, "I have a brother! I have a dog! I have a bedroom! I have a new last name! I have a family!"

That might be the most beautiful picture of adoption I've ever seen, with a powerful connection to our faith. There's a book you can cling to as well, proclaiming the same transformative truths. You have a Father! Because of the death, burial, and resurrection of Jesus, you have a home! Because of Christ, you have a new name! Because of Calvary, you have a family! You have brothers and sisters! Because of the cross, you have a clean slate, a future! Because of the empty tomb, you have new life, both abundant and eternal. You've been saved and you're being sanctified; you've been adopted and now you're becoming like Jesus himself. Hold these truths close to your heart. Never let them go.

In What Way Do You Need God's Rescue?

Through the years I've had the honor of hearing thousands of rescue stories. I don't know your story.

Maybe you're the guy who is successful in every area; you've got the money thing, and the family thing, and the marriage thing, and you still feel alone. Jesus came to rescue you from being isolated. Maybe you're the gal with two thousand friends on Facebook, but you don't have a single real friend who knows you, who loves *you*. Jesus came to adopt you into his family.

Maybe you're the one who has it all together on the outside, but there is something quiet within that isn't all together. Maybe it's anxiety, maybe an eating disorder, maybe a volatile anger, maybe cutting yourself, maybe a struggle with porn or drugs or depression, and you're constantly afraid of that thing. Jesus came to rescue you from you. He rescues you from the rubble and devastating bondage of sin.

Maybe none of these things ring true, but you don't know why you're here on earth. You feel a lack of meaning, of purpose, of identity. Jesus came to rescue you for *life*, abundant and eternal, and bring you into his family.

Will you accept his gift of love? Will you say yes to his rescue? Will you say yes to being adopted into his family? Will you let him bring you home?

May I remind you of the immensity of the love of God the Father? May I remind you of the total, unrelenting, amazing, never-ending, unconditional, unfailing love offered to you through the grace of Jesus? It means this, as Jerry Bridges points out in *The Discipline of Grace*:

> On your worst day you are never out of reach of God's grace.
> On your best day you are never out of need of God's grace.

For rescued messes like you and me, it's all grace, all the time.

MINING THE MESS: **MAKING IT PERSONAL**

Write out some of the powerful implications of grace:

• How does Jesus rescue you? Can you make a list of how completely God rescues you? How often? How many ways?

• Martin Luther talks about how unless you can abuse it, it isn't grace. Grace isn't grace unless it comes with the vulnerability of being able to be abused. What do you think about the radical nature of God's grace? Are there limits to God's grace for you? For others?

• Grace is defined as "undeserved favor." How do you identify with the word "undeserved"? Do you understand this to mean that nobody can lay claim to God's mercy, that none of us deserve his love? How does this make you respond?

• How do you receive God's favor?

• What does God's favor look like in your life?

• How ought this stir our hearts?

• How ought we seek to live in light of its covering?

12

When Vomit Looks like Rescue

And the LORD spoke to the fish, and it vomited Jonah out upon the dry land.

Jonah 2:10 ESV

Forgive me for asking you to picture this scene, but you really can't understand Jonah unless you get your mental imagery kicking in. The fish vomited Jonah up on dry land, and to Jonah, this was a major gift. I know it sounds gross: piles of seaweed, plankton, and a half-digested volleyball that Jonah named Wilson.

To Jonah it was two tickets to paradise. Pack your bags and leave tonight. It was like winning the Powerball lottery plus a lifetime supply of In-N-Out burgers. It was warm water, head-high waves, sunshine smiling, and nothing to do all day but surf and look for a roadside taco stand. Jonah landed in heaven on earth, kissing the ground, hugging Wilson, breathing deep, staring at the sun and praising, praising, praising the God who saved him.

When you let God rescue you, when you surrender to God's plan for your life, God will meet you in your need. What happens next might not sound so nice; in fact, it might sound messy. Having honest, apologetic conversations with friends you've hurt or with family members you've dismissed, or facing your addictions head on—none of it sounds fun, but it is absolutely what your soul needs the most. It might look gross, but it is rescue at work.

As you turn to God, you will be accompanied by joy. You will experience a peace that is unexplainable. You will be ready to face the challenges ahead because you've understood and experienced these same things we see in Jonah: namely, God's rescue. To get out of our glorious mess, we need to keep a few steps in mind. Bluntly, this is how to get the fish to spit you out.

Recognize Where Running Has Led

Look around your heart. Look around your life. Are there places you feel stuck? Discontent? Guilty? Do you sense God calling you toward areas of significant contribution but feel stuck in lethargy? Before Jonah turned, he recognized where he was: "I'm in the bowel of a beast!"

This will require some introspection. We started by identifying large and small ways God is calling us. Now it's time for us to look at specific messes we have caused in our lives by a lack of obedience to God's call. What does God need to rescue you from? What has swallowed you whole? Where has your mess taken you?

Once when my daughter, Alex, was just a baby, I heard her wailing, and it was my turn to check on her, because my wife had made it crystal clear that there was to be no dishing it off again. I stumbled in, groggy, and saw that she had made an absolute mess of things. My cute and gentle two-year-old delight had pulled her diaper off and pulled the sheet off of her mattress, and everything was soaked through. She was lying in a pool of her own production. She was cold and wet and absolutely miserable. I looked at her and said, "Well, you've made your bed. Now lie in it." And I turned off the light and went back to sleep.

No, I didn't. (My wife wouldn't let me. Kidding.) I'm a good dad. I cleaned her up, changed the sheets and her pajamas, and helped her get back to sleep. God is a good dad, infinitely better at fathering than I am. When you cry out to him, in full and sincere recognition of your role in mess making, he responds. He will meet you in the middle of your mess with forgiveness, cleansing, and hope. He will grant you understanding of his love and even wisdom for how you proceed into your potential. Cry out to him. Identify where you have lacked wisdom in your choices.

Return with Humility

Return to God with a humble, repentant heart. How? Return, repent, turn around, run the other direction: all of these are different ways of agreeing with God about your sin. God does not meet our humility with scorn. He's not some petty, vindictive, withholding Soup Nazi in the sky. God is not going to gloat over us ("I knew you'd be back! No soup for you!"). No, God is full of compassion, filled with grace, and offering us mercy.

Recognize where your running has led you, and return. Take refuge in him. Let him be your fortress. I have a buddy who walks in obedience by breathing this mantra to Jesus: "I don't want to look at porn. I just want to look at you." Jesus meets him there and provides strength for the battle. God meets us when we return with humility to him.

Surround Yourself with Support

God has placed some cheerleaders in your world. And I'm not talking braids and bullhorns; I'm talking people who believe in you, people who want your best, people who breathe life into you. Surround yourself with them.

Take the time to cultivate intentional friendships with those you respect, who share your values. It is also wise to build relationships with those who are a few steps ahead of you on the journey of faith. You don't have time to make all the mistakes yourself, so take advantage of the mistakes of others, and learn from them.

I've mentioned a ministry called Celebrate Recovery, which started out of Saddleback Church led by my friend Pastor John Baker. This recovery ministry is based upon Jesus's words in Matthew 5 and has helped thousands walk in freedom, and we've launched a CR ministry at my church in Seattle. Here is why it works: CR offers support, wisdom, and care from someone who knows what it is like to walk in your shoes. Your sponsor is someone who knows what it is like to struggle with your temptations, to wrestle with your addictions. And because they come from a sincere place of support, offering not judgment but the mercy and strength that Jesus offers, you find power for victory. It's the power of godly support in action.

Surrender

Once, when I was a teenager, a sparrow flew inside my house. My younger brother and I were ecstatic. We gleefully tried to chase it out the open doors, but we succeeded only in terrorizing the poor bird. The more we shouted, jumped, and waved our arms, the more the bird was certain we wanted to call it lunch. It darted at each glass window, injuring itself. Finally we got it barreling toward the sliding glass door, but unfortunately it aimed at the glass portion (not the open portion), slammed into it with a thud, and fell dazed onto the floor. With that impact, the bird finally gave up. My brother and I approached it, gently wrapped it in a towel, took it outside, and released it. The sparrow remained still for another moment, unsure. Then it hopped once, then twice, incredulous, and flew away. The bird thought surrender meant destruction, and because of that it nearly destroyed itself. In reality, surrender meant liberation. And the same is true for us.

I fully understand that *surrender* isn't a word Americans like to utter. It makes us feel French. But when it comes to letting God rescue us from our mess, we need to learn how to sound it out. Here is the working definition of surrender: *trusting that God is moving me exactly where I need to be.* The process of surrender is a step-by-step, day-by-day decision. We might make this decision once at a church service or a revival crusade. But surrender is something we choose in daily practice, trusting that God's plans for us are good.

As a part of writing this chapter, I spent some time living this. I recognized some idols: being in control, doing things for the motive of looking good, pursuing my own agenda. I recognized that I was allowing myself to be known, but it was only the well-scrubbed version of me that was on display.

Beware the Scrub

As a follower of Jesus Christ, I seek to live my life consistent with the beliefs that I hold from Scripture. There are times when I live incredibly empowered by God's Spirit. There are times when I stumble and fail. I try to keep short accounts with my wife, short accounts with my brothers, and short accounts with Jesus.

None of this is really where the rub is, and none of this should come as a surprise. Here's where I've been wrestling lately. On my blog, on my Facebook pages, in my messages, I've found myself offering the "well-scrubbed version of me." So while I believe that today's technology offers a clearer way to know one another from a distance than has ever been possible before, I also recognize the potential for hypocrisy that exists. That's why I'm calling it out. Confession is good for the soul.

For example, I scrub myself in photos. The photos I post are typically selected from whole rolls of less exciting photos, plus rolls and rolls of photos that picture me in a combination of unflattering, confused, and rather typical expressions. I try to scrub the boring out, so that a viewer might think, "It must be an amazing adventure to be a part of that clan!" It *is* an adventure, but not nearly as exciting as the posted pictures might suggest. I also choose to post snaps of myself that make me look confident, strong, or handsome. Trust me, these can be really hard to find. The ones with spinach in my teeth I delete.

I also share a ton of family stories. Those are typically the stories that make my kids sound like theologians, my wife sound like a patient genius, and me sound like a great dad, a great husband, and an all-around great guy. All my stories are true (mostly). But what is also true are the stories where my kids fight like siblings, where my wife is tired and short, and where I live closer to dumbness than to greatness.

Even my failures are scrubbed. For example, I might share a time when Jodie was looking for help cleaning the house in preparation for the arrival of guests, while I was upstairs playing Galaga (yes, we have the old arcade version of Galaga, and yes, at Galaga, I am the *man*), and I pretended that I couldn't hear her calling. This "confession" might actually make me sound more holy . . . like, oh look, even Pastor Mike gets a bit selfish sometimes, but he's so awesome for admitting it. But I've scrubbed out the other times during the same weekend when I was already acting selfishly, and how frustrated that must make my wife, and how selfishness is something that I consistently battle to my great chagrin. This paragraph is intentionally hypothetical, but I'm hoping you get the point. A small, safe confession scrubs me too clean.

Now, honestly, I don't think blogs or status updates are the best place to do deep soul work, nor are they the best places for gut-level confession. I don't suggest that to you, nor will I walk that road. The road I walk and recommend involves authentic friendship, accountability, and Christ-centered counseling. But I do want you to beware the scrub. The truth shall set us free.

As I was writing this chapter, I realized that while I might scrub my image, only Jesus can scrub my soul. I prayed, as I want to encourage you to pray,

> Lord, forgive me. I return, I repent, I'm stuck, and I need your rescuing power. Thank you for your grace. Thank you that you understand, and you love me. I surrender to you. Lord, you have never forsaken me. Through stupidity after lunacy after dumb call . . . again and again you are mighty to save. Thank you. Thank you for never giving up on me. Amen.

MINING THE MESS: **MAKING IT PERSONAL**

Submitting to God changes our perspective, our stance, and to illustrate that, I would love to encourage you to get into whatever position feels most right for you: standing, bowing, kneeling, stretching out, arms raised.

Spend some time in prayer with Jesus, speaking out loud to him, and get into a posture that communicates surrender. One of the things that surrender means is that you no longer care about the opinions of those around you; you simply see God, and you see that he is God. And you surrender.

At our church, we do reach our hands toward the heavens as a posture of our reaching up toward the Father who loves us. It's also a symbol of surrender (We cease fighting you, God! We want what you want). I encourage you to do whatever it takes to make your surrender to God real.

(If you're reading this on an airplane, maybe stretching out prostrate before the Lord isn't going to happen right now. But I hope the point is clear all the same. Sometimes our posture informs our hearts of our station before the Lord.)

Seeing God Work

God chose things despised by the world, things counted as nothing at all, and used them to bring to nothing what the world considers important. As a result, no one can ever boast in the presence of God.

1 Corinthians 1:28–29

The bravery of God in trusting us! You say—"But He has been unwise to choose me, because there is nothing in me; I am not of any value." That is why He chose you. As long as you think there is something in you, He cannot choose you because you have ends of your own to serve; but if you have let Him bring you to the end of your self-sufficiency then He can choose you to go with Him to Jerusalem, and that will mean the fulfillment of purposes which He does not discuss with you. We are apt to say that because a man has natural ability, therefore he will make a good Christian. It is not a question of our equipment but of our poverty, not of what we bring with us, but of what God puts into us; not a question of natural virtues of strength of character, knowledge, and experience —all that is of no avail in this matter. The only thing that avails is that we are taken up into the big compelling of God and made His comrades. The comradeship of God is made up out of men who know their poverty. He can do nothing with the man who thinks that he is of use to God.

Oswald Chambers, *My Utmost for His Highest*

13

Thank the God of Second Chances

When I was in high school, I went deep-sea fishing with my dad and brother and reeled in nothing all morning except a sunburn. Everyone got skunked. Near lunchtime my brother decided to lose his breakfast over the starboard side. Always game for a bit of sibling rivalry, I joined him. Suddenly this huge school of oceanic fish appeared out of nowhere, feeding unceremoniously upon our breakfast, apparently delicious the second time around. Less than ten minutes later, the entire boat caught their limit. We should have charged a chum fee.

We fished all morning and all we got was sick. But once we were sick, all we got was fish.

Ironically, that seems to be how God works. When we come to the end of ourselves, when we humbly acknowledge the mess we've landed ourselves in, God delights to pour out his glory in sudden, unprecedented, and unpredictable ways.

If you have ever said to yourself, "I wish I could see God do something amazing"—you can! Not only is this possible, it's what God is calling you to. God desires this for you. This is why we must stop running from him and earnestly seek to obey. When we do that, our messy lives become the canvas for his incredible glory. But the key is thankful living.

Thank the God of Second Chances

Last year, I got a ticket for having expired tags. It was the second ticket in two years I had received for that particular infraction. It might not be the only ticket I've received since moving to Washington. I'm really a good driver. At least that's what I keep telling the police. I went to the court to see if the judge would waive the ticket fee for my expired tabs, since I complied and registered my car immediately. I thought the judge would notice that I was nicely dressed and had a cheerful demeanor and in general conclude that I was good for society. The problem was that she didn't look at me at all; she looked entirely at the computer screen, which I prayed didn't list all of my past infractions. That prayer didn't get answered quite the way I was hoping.

"I see here this isn't the first time you've driven with expired tags."

"No, your honor."

"Looks like you've been busy, Mr. Howerton."

"Yes, your honor." I couldn't think of anything to say that would change my situation. So I blurted out, "I throw myself upon the mercy of the court!" I'm not kidding.

She looked up from the computer screen. Then she smiled and waived the penalty. I was given another chance!

> Then the word of the LORD came to Jonah a second time: "Go to the great city of Nineveh and proclaim to it the message I give you." (Jon. 3:1–2 NIV)

You know what that is called? A second chance. God is the God of second chances (or ten thousandth chances). If this isn't enough to drop us to our knees in humble thanksgiving, I don't know what is!

Mess Begets . . . Masterpiece

No matter where you are, God is offering you a second chance. No matter what you have done, no matter how many times you have done it, no matter where you have wandered, God is saying, "If you invite me to, I'll forgive and forget. If you let me, I'll make it as if it had never happened. If you allow my Son to take it, he will take the stain of your sin and shame and make it white as snow."

Proverbs 28:13 says, "People who conceal their sins will not prosper. But if they confess and turn from them, they will receive mercy."

Another translation of this proverb concludes, "He gets another chance" (TLB).

Picture a white canvas, representing your potential in life. Now imagine you've thrown dark oil paint at it, splattering it with red (symbolizing your murderous selfishness) or charcoal (for your stoic idolatry) or teal (standing for your horrific style choices of the eighties). The paint visually communicates what our sin, our stain, our running from God looks like. We think, "That's it; now I've made a mess of things. It is all I can see. Game over." But it's not. Those simply become the colors that God, the master artist, takes and uses to begin his masterpiece called you.

For this we thank the God of the second chance! When we stop running from him and surrender our lives to him, that's when he does his best work! Accept his grace! Be filled with gratitude! Make a commitment to developing a heart of praise! Leave your pity party behind! Develop a thankful heart! (Use lots of exclamation points!!!)

Building Thanks

Do I really need to be thankful daily for God's second chances?

Is "Absolutely!" a strong enough answer?

Let me paint the concept of perpetual gratitude in this light: What's wrong with the world? I am.

Not that I'm a horrible person or anything. I generally don't break promises, hearts, or windows. I don't steal candy from babies, and every so often, I'll help nice old ladies cross the street. I pay the taxes required of me, I vote, I try to be environmentally conscious, and occasionally I'll hug a tree, a dog, a liberal, or a conservative.

Here is what bugs me: my failure to live up to my own expectations for myself as a human being.

I love my kids, but I have higher expectations of myself as a dad than I'm living now. I provide shelter, food, and relatively stylish clothing; they've got enough toys to set up an eBay business and retire; they've seen *Toy Story 3*, twice. They know I love them, and we wrestle and play with the day's greatest exuberance, but I sense places in myself where I withdraw from the fray because I don't know how to proceed. For example, as my five-year-old son wants to sleep with mommy and daddy for the 784th night in a row, is this a situation for grace or tough love? I don't *know*, and it bugs me. Mostly I err on the side of grace, which means my wife and I have to plan clandestine encounters, and I'm haunted with the vision of raising a spoiled brat who thinks Paris Hilton is modestly appropriate.

Once, in the deep watches of the night, my then two-year-old son was wailing for warm milk, and so I soothed him and brought one right up. Suddenly he's screaming that he doesn't want his milk and I can't make him drink it. So I quieted him and assured him that he had ingested the appropriate amount of calories for the day, and in no regard was I trying to force additional nutrition at 3:00 a.m. I began to leave with the desired and instantly rejected milk, when suddenly it was being called for as a hurricane calls for Florida. Dads don't win battles like that one. They survive, perhaps, yawning and confused, destined to become objects of ridicule by the very spawn they wreck themselves loving. My expectations for myself are so much higher. I expect myself to be the superfather, able to leap the tallest obstacles in life, the one sought for counsel and comfort, the one who imparts strength and confidence, as well as exhibits appropriate humility and a solid work ethic. I pray for my kids to be good, but mostly I pray that prayer for their dad.

Marriage is this whole other deal. My wife is simultaneously patient, beautiful, amazingly good at being a mom, and a fairly consistent source of grace toward a slightly rotter husband. Not that I'm a horrible husband or anything: I'm home nights, I don't drink the paycheck in Guinness, I don't have a temper. But it is no secret that I consistently miss the heart of the issue when it comes to a healthy union. For Christmas years ago, I gave my wife two flannel shirts, each one carefully selected from the early nineties section of my closet (odd fact: it's all early nineties). That wasn't a strong move. Our first year of marriage, I forgot her birthday. Learn from me, people. Last year for Christmas I was thinking of the perfect gift to give my wife, which in my mind is the complete collection of U2 downloaded because I love U2 and how great would that be for me, and suddenly it hit me: I'm the one wrong with the world. Insidiously selfish, even as I work diligently to fight it. Devastatingly thoughtless, even as I seek to be thoughtful. Amazingly hoggish, even as I fashion myself to be a giver.

Grace keeps me alive. Jesus purchased the grace I need on a daily basis. You need this grace too. Everyone does. We don't live up to our own standards, let alone God's standards. God knows that we're a mess. He brings his glory to us in the midst. He provides his grace to move us forward. He is so consistently good, so powerfully forgiving, there is no appropriate response that doesn't begin with thanksgiving. Seeing God work in your life begins with seeing yourself thankful.

Relentless Grace

I recently reconnected with an old friend, Brad, who had mentored me in some early years in my ministry. Several years ago Brad had stepped away from ministry and then revealed that he had failed morally, and an affair cost him his marriage, his reputation, and his ministry. For a while he continued to make poor choices, and as he did so he realized his misery continued to grow. Finally, he stopped running from God. He realized the mess his choices had landed him in. And he simply began, very humbly, to do what God said. He confessed all his sins. He begged forgiveness from all he had hurt with his actions. He broke off the affair and began living in purity, pursuing God's best for sexuality and for life. He began to see a Christian therapist, and he submitted himself to three pastors and another older, mature Christian leader. Working together, they became his restoration team. They met together weekly over the course of eighteen months for study, for accountability, for counsel, and for prayer.

It has been four years since Brad's confession of failure. His ex-wife recently called and forgave Brad for the hurt he had caused her and the family. His girls, both twentysomethings, have expressed forgiveness as well and enjoy a relationship with their dad. And after nearly three years of restoration, the five pastors Brad submitted to unanimously asked him to pray about rejoining God's movement in ministry. They felt that his story and subsequent journey of healing would be encouraging to those who assume God's grace doesn't extend into their mess. Long story short, one year ago Brad launched a church called Life Change Community Church, built on the principle that God can change anybody's life. Life Change, in the first twelve months, has grown to three hundred in attendance, with nearly one-third of those folks experiencing God's grace and giving their lives to Jesus Christ for the very first time. When I was talking with Brad recently, he told me, "God is good, Mike. I'm living proof of grace." He also said that his life verse, the verse that literally fuels his drive daily, is Jonah 3:1: "The word of the LORD came to Jonah a second time" (NIV).

It's true for Jonah. It's true for Brad. And it's true for you.

MINING THE MESS: **MAKING IT PERSONAL**

What are you thankful for? How do you routinely develop and work out your heart of thanksgiving? Some ideas:

• Generate a list of the things about God that you are thankful for. Meditate on his characteristics, his presence, and his Word.

• Build another list of the things about life that you are thankful for. Praise God for your relationships, your circumstances, your blessings.

• Think about the things you face in your life that are hard or difficult. Can you begin to give thanks even in the midst of these messy realities? Read 1 Thessalonians 5:17–19.

• Make a list of the things about yourself (yes, you!) that you are thankful for. Instead of focusing on what is wrong with you in build, in character, or in accomplishment (we routinely examine our defects in detail), spend some time being thankful for what is right. As you do so, realize you're beginning, just a very little bit, to see yourself as God sees you. And this is one more reason to give thanks.

14

How Simple Is It?

God designed faith to have a childlike simplicity. He offers you the gift of his love. Take it. Run in the direction of God's call. Join the adventure. Seeing God work is as simple as seeing yourself obedient to him. He loves you, and his call on your life involves your best as well as his glory. Now, simple might simultaneously mean difficult; however, there are great rewards for simply following God's call, not the least being how your obedience to him brings his kingdom into the here and now.

The writer of Hebrews says Jesus learned obedience through his suffering:

> Even though Jesus was God's Son, he learned obedience from the things he suffered. In this way, God qualified him as a perfect High Priest, and he became the source of eternal salvation for all those who obey him. (Heb. 5:8–9)

You and I are learning obedience in the midst of the mess. The obedience of Jesus provided the source of salvation. Your obedience unlocks that salvation, not only for you but potentially for those who observe you loving God and honoring him with your life.

Simply Available

Jonah has heard God's repeated call, and finally he responds as a servant of God. He obeys. He no longer runs from God but runs toward the things God is heading into. Ultimately, obedience is the mark of a servant. Servants are servants to the degree that they obey their masters. Jonah is reinstated as God's servant:

> Jonah immediately went to Nineveh as the LORD told him. Nineveh was a very large city. It took three days to walk through it. Jonah entered the city and walked for about a day. Then he said, "In forty days Nineveh will be destroyed." (Jon. 3:3–4 GW)

If you have ever doubted whether or not you're eloquent enough, smart enough, or theological enough to share the message of God's desire for a relationship of love, this might be the greatest encouragement you've ever received. Look at Jonah's singular message: "In forty days Nineveh will be destroyed" (v. 4). Not much eloquence. Not many analogies. No cleverness, no testimonies, no modern rock band with a good-looking front man, no PowerPoint, and I'm assuming no CGI explosions. No ethos, pathos, logos; in fact, very little "os" at all. Without debate, it's the worst sermon recorded in Scripture. As my friend Keith says, "The best thing about Jonah's message is its length." If you can't be good, at least be quick.

We don't see eloquence. But what we see is obedience. Just a guy obeying God. Arguably, he was bleached white by the stomach acid in the fish, hairless, and dressed in rags if anything at all, and his voice sounded like it was from beyond the grave (I imagine him looking like the host of *Tales from the Crypt*). But hey, these are just tools God uses.

If God can use that sermon, God can speak through you. Be available to him.

Simply Flawed

I found this quote from Rich Mullins:

> I had a prof one time . . . He said, "Class, you will forget almost everything I will teach you in here, so please remember this: that God spoke to Balaam through his ass, and He has been speaking through asses

ever since. So, if God should choose to speak through you, you need not think too highly of yourself."[6]

God chooses whom he wants to use, and I am amazed God chooses people as obviously flawed and frail as you and me. What he is looking for, I believe more than anything, is humble obedience. And as followers of him, we are to bring a message of love and life that goes beyond the pain and destruction of this world. The world is desperate for this message.

I watched Penn Jillette of Penn & Teller fame and renowned atheist say this on his video blog:

> I don't respect people [Christians] who don't proselytize. I don't respect that at all. If you believe that there's a heaven and hell and people could be going to hell or not getting eternal life or whatever, and you think that it's not really worth telling them this because it would make it socially awkward . . . how much do you have to hate somebody to not proselytize? How much do you have to hate somebody to believe that everlasting life is possible and not tell them that? I mean, if I believed beyond a shadow of a doubt that a truck was gonna hit you, and you didn't believe it, and that truck was bearing down on you, there's a certain point where I tackle you. And this is more important than that.[7]

I love it when an atheist gets on the Christian community for not evangelizing enough. Being willing to share the present and eternal hope we have in the grace of God is part of what we're all called to do. It's why Jonah was called to Nineveh. And it is part of God's call on our lives as well.

Simply Believing

As someone who enjoys surfing, I know that we don't create the waves, we just surf the waves that God creates. Surfers chase waves across the oceans of the planet. They don't set up shop wherever it's cheap and convenient (i.e., Kansas) and wait for God to bring the waves to them. They research, they track, they pursue. What would it look like if we, as followers of Jesus, were this eager to surf the waves that God creates, spiritually speaking? It is obvious that God had already created a wave in Nineveh. It's obvious that he wanted Jonah to surf that wave. This is why God called Jonah in the first place. When Jonah showed up in obedience, God showed up in power.

> The people of Nineveh believed God. They decided to fast, and everyone, from the most important to the least important, dressed in sackcloth. When the news reached the king of Nineveh, he got up from his throne, took off his robe, put on sackcloth, and sat in ashes. Then he made this announcement and sent it throughout the city: "This is an order from the king and his nobles: No one is to eat or drink anything. This includes all people, animals, cattle, and sheep. Every person and animal must put on sackcloth. Cry loudly to God for help. Turn from your wicked ways and your acts of violence. Who knows? God may reconsider his plans and turn from his burning anger so that we won't die." (Jon. 3:5–9 GW)

The whole city was convicted, they believed God, and because they believed, they changed the way they had been living. They took great pains to humble themselves. Sackcloth is a form of burlap that is coarse, scratchy. There's a reason you've never heard the phrase "soft as sackcloth." If hotels didn't want their robes to be stolen, they could make them out of sackcloth. Sitting down in the dust is not something that rulers do with regularity. One contextual insight is that in many courts of antiquity, no one was allowed to be held in higher regard or have a more respected seat than the king. So when the king sits in the dust, the entire population gets dirty bottoms.

Life in Nineveh instantly looked different. Because they believed, lives changed.

Now, let's get gut level honest. A belief will affect the way you live. If it doesn't, then it isn't really a belief. It might be a nice idea, but it isn't a belief. At some point, each of us must decide if Jesus is a pleasant concept, a warm fuzzy, a hazy nicety, or Lord and Savior. We have to decide if we believe. Our faith must be well muscled with action.

Paul never writes about the distinction between faith and works, mostly because he couldn't conceive of people being casual Christians. If you said you were a Christian, you could be burned alive in some emperor's garden or thrown to the lions. First-century believers were rarely casual about their beliefs. So when Paul was walking and preaching and writing and he wrote that faith is what saves, what he meant was a robust, living faith. A faith that was real, vibrant, and bearing fruit.

This is actually why good churches today walk their folks through a membership class and ask those who are committed to sign a covenant.

We don't see membership classes being taught in the first century. When I was a college pastor, occasionally students would ask me, "Why not? Where is the biblical precedent for membership class?" I would respond, "The precedent in the Bible wasn't classes, it was coliseums. They didn't have membership because Christ followers would routinely be murdered. People didn't casually believe, because they knew they could be thrown to the lions, so if a person said they were in, chances were good that they were *really in*. They could count on the church family, and the church family could count on them. Today we tend toward a much more consumeristic view of church. So we have a choice: covenant together as members, or ask Rome to bring the lions back." Membership class never sounded so good.

What Happened to Nineveh

What happened to Nineveh? Nothing. Everything. Nothing bad, that is, and everything good. God saved them. God relented. He offered them grace, the same grace offered to Jonah. He extends to us the same grace he calls us to extend to the world.

God goes nuts over a broken people. Once our hearts are humble and our actions reveal repentance, there is a party in heaven. God pours his grace out on us. God is a compassionate God. God had already shown compassion to Jonah by forgiving him of his rebellion and disobedience. Now we see God's compassion again:

> God saw what they did. He saw that they turned from their wicked ways. So God reconsidered his threat to destroy them, and he didn't do it. (Jon. 3:10 GW)

God had done the work of changing hearts in Nineveh, and for one reason or another God wanted to do his work through Jonah. I don't know why he wanted to use Jonah, but he did. God is doing the work of changing hearts today, and for one reason or another, God wants to do his work through you and me. I don't know why, but he does. The Bible calls us his ambassadors (see 2 Cor. 5:20). God forgives both sinful people and sinful prophets. And he reconciles the repentant to himself.

> I did not come to condemn, but to save! (Jesus's purpose statement; see John 3:17)

God wanted the salvation of the Ninevites, not their destruction. That is what he wants for you, for the world! We can be thankful because God is the God of second chances—for Jonah, for the Ninevites, and for us. In your mess embrace the glorious grace of Jesus. When you realize and celebrate the grace that God has poured out upon you, you'll be free to share it.

MAKING IT PERSONAL: **SIMPLICITY**

• Jesus said that unless we become like a little child, we can't enter the kingdom of heaven. What in the world is he talking about?

• When you think about the journey of following Jesus, do you see it as simple? Why or why not?

• Why have churches insisted on making things so complex?

• Can you write a personal statement of your faith in one paragraph? How about in one sentence? Can you write your statement of faith in six words or less?

• Can you write a personal purpose statement in one sentence?

15

The Bold Choice

I'm a child of the eighties (greatest decade ever). So I'm going to the very pinnacle of cinematic excellence to argue this response to the Lord's grace over us. Of course I'm referring to *The Karate Kid*, starring Ralph Macchio as Daniel, befriended by Mr. Miyagi, wax on–wax off. I didn't see the remake starring Will Smith's kid and Jackie Chan, mostly because . . . how can you improve on perfection?

In a scene when Daniel first begins to train, Miyagi asks him the most important question there is in personal discipline: "Daniel-san . . . are you ready to start learning karate?" "I guess so," Daniel replies. "No, Daniel-san." Miagi pauses. "Karate is like walking down the road. You walk on right side of the road, you're safe. You walk left side, safe. You walk middle, squish. Just like grape. Karate same. You go karate 'yes,' okay. Karate 'no,' okay. You go karate 'guess so,' you get the squish. Like grape."

Brilliant! A halfhearted pseudo-obedience brings nothing but the squish! Mediocrity is the most miserable path of all. (For my Jedi friends, here's the Yoda take on it: "Do, or do not. There is no 'try.'")

Karate Kid Theology

Jesus says the same thing about spiritual status: People who are lukewarm make me nauseous.

141

I know what you have done, that you are neither cold nor hot. I wish you were cold or hot. But since you are lukewarm and not hot or cold, I'm going to spit you out of my mouth. (Rev. 3:15–16 GW)

Growing up, my buddies and I would go cliff jumping in Three Arch Bay in Laguna Beach. There was a ten-foot cliff jump, a thirty-foot jump, and a fifty-five-footer (as judged by kids treading water and looking up, so I'm not certain there isn't a good bit of exaggeration included. But it seemed *huge*). The big one had the air of adventure about it, because the only way to get there was to swim out around the point and then scale the cliff face. As you did, you could see all of the rocks at the base, and you realized you had to run and vault yourself off the top to clear the rocks below. Two problems: there was not much running room (very scary), and the whole thing was covered with ice plant (very slick).

One time my brother, Mark, and two buddies were up there getting up the nerve to jump. Mark's buddy began his vault by running, then lost the nerve and decided to stop suddenly. But he didn't stop. He slipped. And he kept sliding toward the cliff's edge. With eyes bulging out of his head, he continued moving toward the edge, every muscle in his body frozen (except, I understand, the ones controlling his bowels), momentum driving him forward until his feet hung over the cliff. His buddies grabbed him and helped him up, shaken from a near-death experience that he would never forget and I would forever exploit for a sermon illustration. Every mom reading this is thinking, "That's *so* dangerous! I'd never let my kid go cliff jumping." Ah, but if you could overcome your fear and jump, it was absolute glory, holy adrenaline! It was flight into the majesty of creation. (Not to mention, the world's most unforgettable enema. You'd be walking in that reality for a week afterward.) Cliff jumping requires an *all in* commitment. In other words, "Cliff jumping yes, okay. Cliff jumping no, okay. Cliff jumping guess so, *squish*. Just like grape."

Faith is that kind of glory. Be all in. Say, "I will do it, Lord; I will obey your call."

Your Muscle of Choice

Every one of us has an incredible power, which God has given us, called decision. God has given us choice muscles. We don't merely react for self-preservation; we can choose self-sacrifice. It doesn't take a long time to do it, either. Every decision you've ever made to change only took one instant. What takes time is working yourself up to the point where you really are ready to make that decision. I'm challenging you to make a decision today to live in unlimited obedience.

I'm not the first person to challenge like this: Joshua and Moses, great leaders of the Old Testament, both understood this muscle of choice. It doesn't matter if you don't understand how everything is going to play out; you simply decide and then charge ahead. You decide and leap.

Moses says to the children of Israel:

> I have set before you life and death, blessings and curses. Now choose life, so that you and your children may live and that you may love the LORD your God, listen to his voice, and hold fast to him. For the LORD is your life. (Deut. 30:19–20 NIV)

His pupil Joshua says:

> Choose for yourselves this day whom you will serve. . . . But as for me and my household, we will serve the LORD. (Josh. 24:15 NIV)

They understood that a true choice, a firm decision, is an act of obedience in itself.

People who are wishy-washy don't make decisions; they just respond to others' decisions. (You know, the "where do you want to eat, I don't care, where do you want to eat . . . let's eat there . . . okay . . . no, I don't feel like it . . . waaa, waaa, waaa . . . I'm a pathetic human being" kind of people.) A decision means that you have cut off all alternatives. You cut out options, you remove the alternatives, you decide. Decide to follow Jesus. Jump! There's no turning back. You can't undo your decision; you are in. No returning—but why would you want to? What an incredible adventure it is to serve alongside of the God of the universe. What an honor to be colaborers with Christ! All the adventure and glory of cliff jumping, none of the enema.

Giving Generously

I'm going to highlight this with an example of giving generously. Jodie married me fourteen years ago when I was a full-time youth minister making $18,000 a year. I had just received a bump up from $12,000. (Woo hoo! I thought, "I've hit the big time!") Dads, don't let your daughters grow up to marry pastors. They're just as screwed-up as other dudes, but poorer.

But we decided, right from the get-go, that God would receive the first 10 percent of our income and that we wanted to be able to be generous on top of that. God has honored that commitment; God has consistently provided for us and has always allowed us to give at least 10 percent to his church and additional gifts of generosity and blessing on top of that. If you're not living this reality, I want to encourage you to trust God in this. You want to see God's hand in your finances? Take a deep breath, and *jump*!

Recent studies have revealed that Christians in America typically give less today than they did in the worst year of the Great Depression. God is seeing the wealthiest Christians the world has ever known also remain the stingiest. This is an issue of trust versus fear. Fear pushes us to run from God in this regard. My challenge to you is to trust God, and my promise is that in your obedience, he will show you his provision.

There are only four types of people when it comes to giving, and you're one of them: not generous, occasionally generous, regularly generous, and sacrificially generous. Wherever you are, I'd love to challenge you to step out in obedience to the next level. And if you're one of those sacrificially generous folks, even though I don't know you, here's what I can deduce: you are where you are because you have already stepped out in courageous obedience, and you've discovered that you can't outgive God. Right? When you realize God moves through our obedience, it builds a hunger for greater obedience!

Inspired Coaching Inspires Excellence

I played high school football under two powerful men I respected, Coach Crow and Coach Rush, and it was interesting to see how they had the good cop, bad cop thing down brilliantly. We'd be behind at halftime, and our head coach, Coach Crow, would come in growling, spitting disdain in his words at us: "What a bunch of losers, whaddya say let's get your girlfriends suited up, they'd do a better job, your flimsy arm-tackles make me wanna puke, I'm gonna go look for some diapers for you babies to wear in the second half, maybe then you won't embarrass yourselves so bad." He'd leave and absolute silence would descend; virtually no sound except for the muffled sobs of Monty, our kicker, in the corner.

Then our defensive head coach, Coach Rush, would come in. He'd look each of us in the eyes with his steely glint. When he began to speak, you could *feel* strength flow into your limbs. He would begin with something like this, measured, masculine, and building in intensity: "I don't see high school students. I see lions. This locker room is filled with lions. A bunch of lions is called a *pride*. A pride of lions hunts together. A pride of lions kills together. Lions show no mercy. Lions are majestic to behold. Lions terrify their prey. Lions are the kings of the land, and this *is* your land. *You* are the pride here. But there's one thing I haven't heard you lions do tonight. I haven't heard you roar. Now we're gonna go out there, and your opponents, and everyone in the stands, and everyone in this two-bit town is gonna hear you roar because you are LIONS and LIONS ROAR!" And we'd erupt in an ear-splitting roar (even Monty) because we weren't seniors or juniors, we were LIONS and LIONS ROAR, and we'd go out to inevitable victory (but you probably read about that in the papers). When Coach Rush died unexpectedly a few years later, he was so beloved that there was a motion to name the stadium after him.

What kind of coach do you want? With culture as your coach, your false gods are sneering at you in your weakness. But when you allow Jesus Christ to be your Lord and Savior, when he is calling the plays in your life, you will be more, you will live more, and you will have greater significance than you can imagine. Jesus is inspiring, empowering, noble, beautiful; let him call the plays in your life. Obey him.

MINING THE MESS: **MAKING IT PERSONAL**

I don't know what areas of courageous obedience God is prompting you to specifically in your life, because I don't know where you're not currently obedient. He might be calling you to higher levels of purity, of sharing his grace, or of serving in his church. But I want to highlight one area where I know Jesus has a call on your life.

He's calling you to give to his kingdom. The Word talks about financial faithfulness in the Old Testament and radical generosity in the New Testament. Jesus upped every single legal command, moving it to a heart issue between ourselves and God. ("You've heard it said, 'No adultery.' Right. But I also say, 'No lust.'") By focusing on our hearts instead of the law, he upped the ante. The same is true with finances. He doesn't want to hold the tithe (10 percent) up as a pinnacle but rather merely a starting point. Jesus makes a big deal about the sacrificial giver. He elevates the widow who gives to God everything she had to live on.

This exercise is simple: whatever level you're at in terms of your giving, crank it up a notch.

Courageously tell God you'll trust him, and give to his kingdom exactly what he's calling you to give. Commit to this lifestyle for the next twelve months, and watch how God meets you in this adventure! In your courageous obedience, you will see God work. You're a lion. It's time to roar.

16

Finding Joy

Jonah finally obeyed God's call on his life, and 120,000 people were saved. That is some Harvest Crusade. A reluctant prophet finally stopped running and simply did what God told him to. The results were overwhelming. He saw God work. If you are interested in living in that kind of joy as you see God's hand moving in the world through your life, the first thing to keep in mind is that God's plan is infinitely better than mine.

From Gelda to Golden

I used to date a girl we'll call Gelda. This girl would have curdled milk. She had the ability to suck the life out of any conversation with arrogance, manipulation, or sulking. She was an absolute personality disaster for Mike Howerton. I'm not saying she isn't perfect for somebody. Everybody is perfect for somebody. (Hitler's gone, bin Laden's unavailable, but there's somebody out there for her. I exaggerate. But not much.) The funny thing is that when we were dating, I was praying to God that he would bring us closer together, that he would allow us to up our level of commitment (while I was typing that I had a little gag reflex). Like Garth Brooks, sometimes I thank God for unanswered prayers.

This last Friday night we enjoyed family night in the Howerton home. I heard laughter and squealing upstairs, and suddenly my children came barreling down for our movie night, all jammied up. My daughter, Alex, jumped on my lap and kissed me on the smacker; my wife, Jodie, sat next to me, holding my boys who are mischief incarnate; the fire was crackling; we were eating popcorn together; and the dog was nowhere to be seen. That's as close to golden as it gets down here on this fallen planet!

And honestly, I thought to myself, *How good is God, that he had this in store for me!* There's Mike, praying for Gelda, daughter of Stalin, and God says no, instead giving me a Norman Rockwell scene. Because God's plan is so much better than our plan, we can live with joy.

The second thing to remember is that joy is one of the by-products of being his. He plants it and grows it within us:

> But the fruit of the Spirit is love, joy, peace, patience, kindness, goodness, faithfulness, gentleness, self-control; against such things there is no law. (Gal. 5:22–23 ESV)

Happiness is built upon the happenings around us, but joy is built upon the Spirit of God in our lives. The more we are filled and fueled by God's presence, the more joyfully we will live, because joy is his idea.

The third thing to keep in mind is that God is doing great things through us. God is doing great things through our obedience, in the lives of others and in our own lives. This is a current reality. God *is* working through you. Go back to your active listening of God's call in your life. Recall that book he is prompting you to write? Remember those friends you long to lead to Jesus? That ministry he is calling you to start at your church? The moment you decide to follow his call and act to do so, he meets you and begins to work through you. Even the first steps you are walking toward fulfilling God's call on your life, he will use to encourage others. In fact, you are inspiring people right now, and you don't even know it.

> Therefore, my dear brothers and sisters, stand firm. Let nothing move you. Always give yourselves fully to the work of the Lord, because you know that your labor in the Lord is not in vain. (1 Cor. 15:58 NIV)

What does it mean to "give yourselves fully"? It means living in courageous, joyful obedience. What does it mean that your work in the Lord is "not in vain"? It means God is using you, right now, right where you are, to impact others for his name's sake, to touch others with his love.

God Invites *Us* into His Story

You need to commit this truth to memory: "God invites me into his story." Write it on a Post-it. Stick it on your dashboard. Staple it to your Schwinn. Shave it on the side of your pug. Tattoo it on your forehead, backward (so you can read it in the mirror). You are invited into God's story.

And don't get too wrapped up in needing immediate gratification. If you invite someone to come with you to church and they blow you off, don't take it personally. If you begin a spiritual discussion and they change the subject, don't be discouraged. If you reach out in love to someone and they reject you, your first natural response may be to withdraw and write them off, but don't allow your heart to hit the downward spiral. Keep your joy, despite an apparent lack of results. Our labor for God is never, never in vain. I've been doing ministry long enough to know that planting seeds produces a harvest, even when you can't see it.

Over many years of ministry I've seen some incredible things, but most of the time, not instantly. In my first youth ministry, I met a young gal named Misty, spelled funky with a silent *j* shoved in the middle of her name, and maybe an umlaut (Mystje? Myjstee?). She was pierced and tatted and had a horrific story of pain and family brokenness. She was befriended by my wife and some other volunteers in our ministry, spent the better part of a school year in our ministry, and connected in a small group. She served with us on a short-term mission trip to Mexico. And then near the end of the year, she was gone. Student leaders and her small group leader followed up . . . no response. I called her. No response. At the time I was in the habit of sending out a printed postcard about once a month to students in our group. We made them in house on blue cardstock, and they just said "I prayed for you today." I'd write a quick note and send it off. So I shot Misty a postcard and was pretty sure I put the *j* in the wrong place. I didn't hear back. It seemed she had fallen off the planet.

About four years later, I was serving as the college pastor of Saddleback Church, and in walked Misty. And she was radiant. She had this smile—you could see she was living with joy. She told me a brief synopsis of her life: she got into hard drugs, went to live with her deadbeat dad in another state, was hanging out with folks who were horrible for her, and had even gone through the pain of an abusive relationship, pregnancy, and abortion. She had packed a ton of devastation into her life in four years. But in her despair she had turned her life over to Jesus. She got healthy, got clean, found a good church, and was living as a joyful follower of the King. I was so glad to see her, and it was easy to see that God had touched her. Then she reached into her purse and pulled out this crumpled blue postcard.

She handed it to me, grinned, and said, "You put the *j* in the wrong place. Remember this?" I read it. It said on the front: "I prayed for you today." And then I saw on the back a note in my handwriting: "Jesus loves you like crazy, Mystje, and I think you're pretty cool too. Hope you're well . . . Come back soon, because you're missed. Mike."

She said, "I tacked this on the wall right next to my bed. There were nights my life was spinning out of control on substances, or nights when I felt literally dead inside with the devastation of my sin. But then I'd glance at this postcard, and I remembered that somebody out there missed me, that somebody out there was praying for me. In my darkest moments, I want you to know, it was like a lifeline for me."

God blows me away! That thoughtfulness cost me very little. But it made a very *big* difference. And although I'm about instant gratification, God is so often about walking with us on a journey. I can have joy because God is using my life right now, and he's using yours as well.

Riches Beyond the Rules

We live joyfully because the things God commands us to do are for our absolute best. His call on your life is for his glory and for your best. Being joyful in our obedience to God's plan is much easier when you have the right perspective. Many people only see the "rules" of Christianity, and that's all they think God cares about—rules like, "don't join the mob," "never take the tag off a mattress," "never ask a woman if she's pregnant." But the "rules" are simply the groundwork for not destroying your life. God has far, far more than that in store for you: infinite goodness, vast significance, and his glory as well.

Think about the analogy of driving. You are just getting your license, and so you study the manual, where you are told you should avoid telephone poles, not drive on sidewalks, and probably get AAA. Not very exciting stuff, but it keeps you alive. However, those are just the basics. It doesn't even begin to cover how to take a road trip from Nome, Alaska, to Tierra Del Fuego, Chile, or how to rent a motorbike in Europe for pennies and see the entire continent in two months of glory! (If the open road excites you, I'd love to get you my first book, *Miles to Cross*. It's about travel, spiritual and geographical, and it sold like seventeen copies. My mom has a box in her garage. They're about a quarter on Amazon.)

God's plan for you includes some basics, because he loves you and doesn't want you to experience pain, and that's where the rules fit in, but that is simply the beginning. God's plan for you means a personal journey. It is life on the pinnacles of existence; it is wonder and joy and amazement. It's a discovery of you tapping into the best and brightest parts of yourself in order to contribute something to God's kingdom that only you can contribute. Do we get how good it is to follow hard after God? Do we understand that the highest, fullest, richest life is available in *him*?

This is how we see God work in our lives. We simply obey God with thanksgiving and joy. We don't obey in order to earn God's love, but we obey because of the incredible love God has shown us. Jesus has proven his love for us. When we obey him, we reveal our love for him. Jesus says, "If you love me, you will obey what I command" (John 14:15 NIV 1984).

Remember the analogy of that canvas spattered with the stains of your disobedience? Now imagine seeing it after God has been working on it. Imagine the artist turns his craftsmanship toward you, and you see that it's a beautiful masterpiece God has been painting with your life. You will see the character that he produced in you: the character of thankfulness, of courageous obedience, and of joyful living. You will see the emergence of the character of Jesus Christ. You will see the darkest places in your journey have become the relief against which his grace shines. And you will discover that the areas of your struggle and brokenness have become the place of his great victory and your great ministry. Your mess showcases his glory.

Oh, and you probably *should* get AAA.

MINING THE MESS: **MAKING IT PERSONAL**

• How does our joy get stolen?

• What are some of the differences between joy and happiness?

• How do we increase our happiness?

• How do we fuel our joy?

• When you're in need of a joy boost, what are some things you focus on?

• Rewrite the following psalm in your own words:

> I take joy in doing your will, my God,
>   for your instructions are written on my heart. (Ps. 40:8)

Embracing God's Amazing Grace

So then, since we have a great High Priest who has entered heaven, Jesus the Son of God, let us hold firmly to what we believe. This High Priest of ours understands our weaknesses, for he faced all of the same testings we do, yet he did not sin. So let us come boldly to the throne of our gracious God. There we will receive his mercy, and we will find grace to help us when we need it most.

Hebrews 4:14–16

I often dream that I am tagging along behind Jesus, longing for him to choose me as one of his disciples. Without warning, he turns around, looks straight into my eyes, and says, "Follow me!" My heart races, and I begin to run toward him when he interrupts with, "Oh, not you; the guy behind you. Sorry."

Michael Yaconelli, *Messy Spirituality*

Grace is love, but love of a special sort. It is love which stoops and sacrifices and serves, love which is kind to the unkind and generous to the ungrateful and undeserving. Grace is God's free and unmerited favour, loving the unlovable, seeking the fugitive, rescuing the helpless, and lifting the beggar from the dunghill to make him sit among princes (Ps. 113:7, 8).

John Stott, *Authentic Christianity*

17

When Grace Isn't Wanted

Fly-fishing is a thing of great loveliness. Its arcing movements are majestic. Every cast is haiku. John Eldredge seems to suggest that it goes with masculinity like arm hair, body odor, and a Zeppelin collection. (To be fair, I asked John about this at his boot camp last May, and he denied it. That was right before he and his team duct taped my butt cheeks together. I kid. I kid.) But if you have never gone fly-fishing, you need to know that it's actually quite difficult to pull off. If you have gone fly-fishing, then you know I'm understating my case. My dad tried to teach me. I watched *A River Runs through It*. Even so, when I cast, all I catch is a snarl.

What I'm trying to say is that appreciating something and living it are two completely different kettles of fish. Knowing the road is different from walking the road. And sometimes we have to be taught the same lessons again and again.

Here we are at the end of the book of Jonah. It's been quite a ride. You might think that after seeing 120,000 people turn to the one true God in humble repentance, Jonah would be singing, "I am the world's greatest evangelist!" and jumping up and down, nutty with joy. "What are you going to do now, Jonah?" a reporter shouts over the crowd. "I'm going to Disneyland!" he yells back. He gives the peace sign, yells "Hi, Mom!" and ducks into a limo with paparazzi camera flashes popping right and left.

Not our Jonah.

But it displeased Jonah exceedingly, and he was angry. (Jon. 4:1 ESV)

The Hebrew literally states, "It was evil to Jonah with great evil." Jonah was, how shall we say, bumming supremely. Does God use people who are emotional roller coasters? Yes. I guess this is slightly understandable. I've been emotional after missions and ministry mountaintop experiences too. Look at Elijah. Elijah had this incredible mountaintop experience. He was in the front row on Mount Carmel, watching God kick some serious Baal booty (that too is the literal Hebrew), hundreds of false prophets losing the altar cook-off contest and being slaughtered the same day, and yet the next time we see our victorious Elijah, he's hiding in a cave, feeling defeated and wishing he were dead. Life is a bit of an emotional roller coaster. The Bible knows it, and so do you.

Go Get 'Em, God!

God wired us up. He knows our emotional gearshifts. But because God knows how we are wired, he also knows that not all of our emotions are legit—sometimes they are the result of a wrong focus. This is true in Jonah's case:

> So he complained to the LORD about it: "Didn't I say before I left home that you would do this, LORD? That is why I ran away to Tarshish! I knew that you are a merciful and compassionate God, slow to get angry and filled with unfailing love. You are eager to turn back from destroying people." (Jon. 4:2)

God's grace isn't a problem when we are the recipients. But it can be a problem when he offers grace to people who annoy us. It becomes a bigger problem when God wants to offer grace to those who anger us. Remember, the Ninevites were the bad guys. God had no covenant with the dirty Assyrians, but God spared them anyway. The word in this passage that's translated as *compassion* is the same word that describes the caring love and tender grace a mother has for her child. That's what God was expressing toward Nineveh. Jonah is right. God is a God of grace. God is slow in anger. God is abounding in love. And Jonah doesn't like it! This is unwanted grace. Even though Jonah is a recent recipient of God's amazing grace, he balks when God decides to grace Jonah's enemies. He wants a "Go get 'em" God.

> "Just kill me now, LORD! I'd rather be dead than alive if what I predicted will not happen." The LORD replied, "Is it right for you to be angry about this?" (Jon. 4:3–4)

Reputation's Place

"Are you *right* to be angry," God asks, "or are you wrong in your focus?" Jonah is essentially saying, "I'd rather be dead than alive because nothing I predicted is going to happen." Jonah is concerned over his reputation. Now, according to Deuteronomy 18:21–22, he has good reason to be concerned: a false prophet was identified when just one of his prophecies failed to come true. Just one. It ran the risk of capital punishment. Jonah prophesied that Nineveh would be overturned in forty days. Now it doesn't look like it is going to happen. So reputation is a big deal for him. We don't have anything like the same pressure Jonah might have felt, yet how many of us are concerned about our reputation?

A heightened concern for our reputation prevents us from living the wide-open life that follows God's call joyfully. People sometimes think that following God's will automatically makes them a nut. They think the moment you say yes to Jesus, you suddenly start wearing more faith-based paraphernalia than Stephen Baldwin: Christian shirts, Jesus hats, fish stickers on your possessions, and WWJD bracelets on all appendages. And that it's a requirement to check half your brain at the door. When I was in high school, Huey Lewis and the News came out with a song called "Hip to Be Square," and many Christian movements embraced it as a theme, like "Look at us . . . we're the dorks of the world!" I wasn't interested (in a movement of nerdiness, that is; obviously, Huey Lewis is a genius).

That isn't what God wants for us. He wants us to live vibrant, unpolluted, joyful, and attractive lives being *his* and by doing so attract others to his love. We can simply be ourselves, neither fearful of working for the approval of men nor intentionally scorning a good reputation. But God's opinion is the one we care most about. Paul writes:

Obviously, I'm not trying to win the approval of people, but of God. If pleasing people were my goal, I would not be Christ's servant. (Gal. 1:10)

Yet Jesus is described as growing in wisdom and stature, in favor with both God and men (see Luke 2:52). So it is possible to be both godly and well-respected. We can be both winsome to others and faithful to God. But our chief concern should be our standing with God. Where is your priority? Are you more caught up with your reputation in your world or your relationship with him?

MINING THE MESS: **MAKING IT PERSONAL**

- Are there times when God offers grace to people we wish he wouldn't? When was the last time the thought of God's grace caused you to be a bit uncomfortable?

- Read the parable of the unmerciful servant in Matthew 18:21–35. In this teaching, what is Jesus telling us about our need of God's grace? What does it say about God's desire that we share his grace with others?

- Do you think Christians in general have a reputation for being graceless or grace-filled? Which word would you imagine someone using to describe you?

- Have Christians in your community earned a good or a bad reputation? How have they earned it?

- How do you think it's possible for believers to be both respected in their communities and faithful to God's call?

18

Building Your Life on God's Grace

I know I'm a pastor, but I'm a human being too. I have every fear, every hesitation that you might have. When I bring up spiritual conversations with my friends and neighbors and the guys I coach Little League baseball with who don't have faith, my heart pounds a bit. It's not an easy thing to bring up Jesus or have conversations about church when our culture affirms literally every other topic but labels this one taboo. All I know is that we can't afford to be silent. We cannot care more of what others think than what God thinks.

Because of this, it truly matters what you're building your life on. This, by the way, will be your reputation.

You Only Get One

Now I know that we haven't thought obsessively about this since junior high, but we all are actively building our reputation on some concept. We're all building the foundation of our lives, and what we build upon is what we are going to be known for. You might be building your reputation on your good looks, your clever antics, your wisdom in the stock market, your knowledge of *Lord of the Rings* trivia, or something else. But we all are conscious of what others think about us. When it comes to God's grace, we begin by moving the focus off ourselves.

It is an interesting paradox. The more you focus on your reputation (keeping up with the Joneses, being cool, wearing the right clothes, having the right gadgets, hanging with the right crowd), the more your reputation suffers. It is a bit like climbing an unstable ladder. You might make it to the top, but that would be the least secure place of all. This will only bring out the worst in you as far as being needy or relying on someone else's approval. And it doesn't serve the kingdom of God at all.

Focusing on God's grace for you liberates you from this. The paradox is that when you take the focus off yourself and place it on the needs of your friends, co-workers, or neighbors—when you stop caring about what they think of you and start just caring about them—you'll find that they think well of you.

Rick Warren said via Twitter, "To develop friendships, stop trying to be interesting and just be interested in others."[8]

And Paul said via letter (which was a very early beta test of Twitter), "Let each of you look not only to his own interests, but also to the interests of others" (Phil. 2:4 ESV).

Boycotting Boycotts

Chances are you can only build your life on one platform, and it takes years to build. You can destroy a reputation in an instant, but you build it over the long haul. What do you *want* to be known for? What *are* you known for?

Christians in general are known in our culture for all sorts of things: intolerance, sexual shenanigans, financial impropriety, and sweater vests.

I realize this and go: *Wait a minute!* I want to be part of *another* movement! I want to be part of the movement where Christ followers are known for hosting the greatest parties. Where Christians are known for caring profusely about their neighbors. Where Christians are known for loving Jesus practically, sponsoring the care of millions of vulnerable children around the planet, replenishing food banks, and financing microbusiness loans. The number of churches in America is larger than the number of orphans in America. If just one couple in every fourth church in our nation would follow God's call to adopt, there would be no orphans. No more orphans. Can you imagine that story hitting the CNN home page? "Remember how there used to be orphans in America until the *church* stepped up?" Can you imagine how that would build the reputation of Christ in our nation?

A previous church I served was part of a denomination, and the head of that denomination (the president or protestant pope or the pastoral prime minister—I'm not really sure of his *exact* title) at one point in his tenure declared that every church and every member of every church in his denomination needed to boycott Disneyland.

At my church when the decree was issued, the other pastors and I looked at each other, raised our eyebrows, and thought about it for like half a nanosecond. We concluded, *Not a chance*, for two reasons: first, since it was nearby, most of the pastors on staff had season passes to Disneyland. Second, none of us wanted to be known as the church that boycotts the happiest place on earth.

You only get one. You can only be known for one thing. If you seek to build your life on control, you give up building a reputation on freedom. If you seek to build on conditional acceptance, you forfeit building on unconditional love. If you build a life on what you're against, you'll lose the chance to build it on what you're for.

Early on in my ministry, a sincere man grabbed me and talked to me about using my passion and my platform to sell Amway products. Now, I've got nothing against Amway, which has provided a good life for a lot of folks, but I respectfully told him no (and not because I thought it would infringe upon my Mary Kay business).

I said, "I've got one pitch. I want to make my pitch 'Jesus.'" Right now, my church has one chance to land in the imagination of the Northwest culture, one reputation to build, and I want my pitch to be "Jesus." I'm a "Jesus loves you!" kind of guy. Overlake Christian Church is a community where lives are transformed as people find and follow Jesus. We live as a family of Jesus followers who love God, love people, and serve the world. That's the platform. We open Scripture to discover how.

"But you didn't say anything about praying for Israel." No, but John Hagee says that a ton, in lots of podcasts; it's simply not our gig. "But you didn't say anything about politics." Nope, but Dobson's been holding court for years; that's his thing. Our gig is Jesus. "But you didn't say anything about being amazingly, ridiculously, absurdly happy." No, but google Joel Osteen. That's his gig, and he's good at it. Our gig is Jesus.

Our one thing is going hard after Jesus because Jesus is the only one who provides the grace each one of us continually needs, the grace each one of us fails to earn.

Add this to the list of important theologies Jonah missed. He failed to realize how he was a recipient of God's grace, and he failed to offer grace to Nineveh. He neglected dealing with his own sense of judgment, and he failed to let God be the one building his reputation. This is what happened:

> Jonah left the city and sat down east of it. He made himself a shelter there. He sat in its shade and waited to see what would happen to the city. (Jon. 4:5 GW)

He was still hoping for the fire and brimstone! He didn't get God's heart. Jonah was sitting on the Assyrian plain, 115 degrees Fahrenheit in the scarce shade, wanting to see God's destruction, but instead all he saw was a people sitting in the dirt, fasting, dressing their cows and pugs up in burlap sweaters. Jonah saw the economic expansion of the sackcloth clothiers of Nineveh. He wanted to see their destruction, but instead he witnessed their salvation. God had chosen to show mercy to a wayward people and a wayward prophet, but Jonah couldn't see past his own judgment. He had written them off. He didn't want them to change, nor did he want to change. Jonah was finding fault with God. He wanted God to be all wrathful and strong and kicking some Mesopotamian behind.

But that isn't God's ultimate desire.

MINING THE MESS: **MAKING IT PERSONAL**

• What is your life built upon?

• How do you currently take pains to build a reputation? What are some of the things you feel Jesus is prompting you to pursue so that they are a part of your reputation?

• Did Jonah have a point? Are there limits to God's grace?

• The national news recently covered a family from a small church in the Midwest who show up at funerals for United States soldiers killed in action. The purpose of their presence at these memorials is to hold hand-painted protest signs about homosexuality, the effect of which is to make God look like a hatemonger. How does the news coverage of this family impact the reputation of all followers of Jesus? How does this impact the reputation of God and his grace?

• What would it look like in your life to let God build your reputation? How do you think a church gains a reputation in a community?

19

God's Ultimate Desire

God's ultimate desire is to adopt a people to himself. His desire is grace.

I had lunch with a friend of mine a while ago, and we saw a woman walking through the restaurant. She was older, kind of mean looking, with jet-black hair, and my friend told me he had seen her a few moments earlier as we were coming in. He noticed she was wearing a large pentagram necklace. A pentagram is a symbol commonly honored by those who are interested in the occult or by Satanists. And my friend confessed that as he saw this scowling woman and her pentagram, his first response in his heart was, "The devil can have her." As soon as he said it, he realized what a fool he was, and immediately he began to pray for her. He also prayed for himself, that he would have the character of grace for all, even those who were currently diametrically opposed to God, because anyone can change. I did.

When Church Works

When church works, it looks something like this: revealing a grace so vast none can fully exclude themselves from it; a discipleship so rigorous none can fully include themselves in it; a love so close, so overwhelming, so mysterious none can begin to explain it, save that

Jesus is present here, enticing a spiritually starving, junk food generation to his banqueting table. Jesus is present, wooing an adulterous
and lust-sick people to his satisfying intimacy and our deep fulfillment. Jesus is glorified, leading a stumbling-through-the-dark, lost,
alone, and frightened humanity into the warmth of his illuminated
embrace. When church works, it is light for the road. When it works,
it produces God's ultimate desire and celebrates grace.

But Jonah just doesn't seem to get it, so God becomes a children's
pastor and gives him an object lesson:

> The LORD God made a plant grow up beside Jonah to give him shade
> and make him more comfortable. Jonah was very happy with the plant.
> At dawn the next day, God sent a worm to attack the plant so that it
> withered. When the sun rose, God made a hot east wind blow. The sun
> beat down on Jonah's head so that he was about to faint. He wanted
> to die. So he said, "I'd rather be dead than alive." Then God asked
> Jonah, "What right do you have to be angry over this plant?" Jonah
> answered, "I have every right to be angry—so angry that I want to
> die." (Jon. 4:6–9 GW)

Now, this chapter could also be called, "How to Care More about
People than Shrubbery" or "How to Stop Being an Absolute Whiner,"
but I like "The Day God Gave Me Worms." Jonah is topping the charts
with his world-class pity party.

God tries to help Jonah shift his perspective by providing a shade,
a worm, a scorching wind; this same God provided a storm and a fish
and a call on the prophet's life. One thing it is important to see is just
how involved God is in the events of our lives. Think about that for a
second: God is involved in your daily life. The question "What is God
teaching me through this?" might be the most important question we
can ever ask. We probably can never ask it too often. God is involved
in your daily life. That truth amazes me. The Lord of the universe is
involved in your hourly routine. When you hit your alarm clock and
ate your Pop-Tarts and tried to drive to work but it was raining and
your car wouldn't start so you had to call your buddy for a ride, God
was in it. He was there. He was involved and wondering when you
would turn to him.

Again Jonah wishes he were dead. For the second time. He's throwing another tantrum, ready to die because a vine is now gone. I think
to myself, "What a whiner. Snap out of it, fish bait!" Listen, before
we get too smug here, what are some of the things that make us

absolutely freak out? Where do we get discouraged because we are focusing solely on ourselves?

In other words, where are you being inappropriately sensitive? When you hit an obstacle, do you weep in despair? When a person looks at you weird, do you think you must be unlovable? If you get a speeding ticket, do you think there is a government conspiracy out to get you? (There is. I'm sorry. I've said too much already.)

One day I woke up early and had a great time with God. I spent some time reading his Word. I spent some time journaling my prayers. I felt like God met me there and filled me with joy. Then, as I was about to leave the house, my wife informed me that I had forgotten to pay a bill, and now we had a late fee. Suddenly my joy was gone! I was a failure as a human being. Clearly I didn't deserve to be alive if I couldn't remember to pay bills on time. Fortunately God broke through my overly inflated recriminations and reminded me that I'm his child, with or without having to pay late fees. We paid the bill. I went to work. The world didn't end.

Sometimes God is teaching us through a circumstance, and other times he's using you to teach someone else. He's working on you, but he's also working through you. Take a deep breath. Relax. Contrary to what it might seem like in the moment, the universe is not revolving around you. That is where Jonah's focus was—inappropriately on himself. When we're there, God says, "You don't have my perspective. My desire is grace."

Puppy Love

My wife was so in love with this little black puppy, holding it like it was a child of prophecy, a wiggling child with a psycho tongue that licked her face like it was covered in A1 Steak Sauce. I was a goner. We named him Bilbo, since he was a runtish, wrinkled thing, and his middle name was Ugly, mostly for the same reason. He was a purebred pug, which means nothing to anyone but me, since it was a fact that excused the store to ravage my checking account. But I'm so glad he was purebred, since we've shown him at several dog shows and bred him with other purebreds and so seen a handsome return on our ugly pet. Oh, wait, we didn't do these things, because we had a life, or kids rather.

When my wife and I were pre-kiddos, Bilbo was our baby. He slept in our bed. He got baths often, ate food from our table, went on multiple walks a day, and heeled so obediently that he didn't use a leash. He was a prince. Then my daughter was born. He became a dog. Then my son was born. He became a nuisance. It is amazing what sleep deprivation and a chaos level that was consistently above the threshold of sanity will do. Bilbo had a yard. He had a bed (in the garage). We fed him regularly. But he had fallen from the glory days of youth, or we had fallen from the glory days of ownership, and he wasn't happy about it.

Turns out, Bilbo knew exactly what to do to get a little more attention. They say that teenagers will choose negative attention over no attention, and Bilbo had learned from them. He began to seek out unusual places to relieve himself. Off-limits places. Like, inside my shoes. In my wife's closet. Behind the couch. You get the picture.

Discipline didn't seem to work. Punishment didn't faze him (he had a hard, ugly pug heart, this one). So I began to walk him again. Daily. Many days, multiple times. We began to care for him as we had done in the golden era of puppy yore.

The Ten-Thousand-Dollar Dog

But because Bilbo was now much older, and potentially incontinent, and had trained himself to go to the bathroom in the nice, cozy, warm closets and bedrooms of our home, the "accidents" continued. I don't mind telling you that I thought many less-than-pastoral things as I cleaned up after him. Jesus taught us to love our enemies, but honestly, he never owned a pug. Not to mention that Bilbo was beginning to cost us serious coin. He ran out in the street and had a tangle with a neighbor's car . . . *cha-ching*. He had a tendon in his leg that needed to be reattached with surgery . . . *cha-ching*. Suddenly he has allergies that require us (and by "us," I'm assuming you know I mean "my wife") to inject him regularly with some kind of canine antisneeze, antiscratch formula . . . *cha-cha-cha-ching*. And then he gets this cancerous growth on his paw, and we're looking at another surgery and biopsy and I don't know what else . . . chemo? I'm picturing my pug bald and wrinkly and nauseous (going projectile in addition to the regular gifts he hides for us to find). For this much money, no kidding, I could put in a pool. I'm bitter, I'm broke, and I'm frustrated with this smelling, sneezing, squatting pug who considers himself a king in exile.

As we take this living bane of my home-life existence to the vet and the vet begins to tell us the level of *cha-ching* we can expect to suffer, I see my daughter get down on her knees, hug the dog tightly, and say, "It's all right, buddy. We're going to fix you up." And she looks up at me with tears in her eyes, and I'm not surprised to see them, but I am surprised to notice the tears blurring my eyes as well. I love my family. And Bilbo is a part of my family. And I realized that means I love him too. I don't know honestly how much longer we're going to finance his medical miracles, because he is old, and there surely is a point we're approaching sooner rather than later where hospice begins to sound good not only to us but to him as well.

But the realization that I love Bilbo is a big deal to me. I love the thing that produces soft, rancid Easter eggs and hides them in my dirty clothes. I love the thing that smells because of his skin allergies, the thing that is costing me an arm and a leg, the thing that promises to cost me as long as he lives. And I love him still, and I choose to care for him and clean up after him and make him as comfortable as possible. Because that's what family means.

He Gives More Grace

The point of this dog tale is that I know I must be a whole lot like Bilbo to God. I keep leaving messes around the place. I keep stinking the place up. I've got quirks, shortcomings, all sorts of entitlement fantasies. I keep marking my territory. James 4:6 tells us that God gives us *more* grace. I don't doubt that God gets fed up with me, that his love is filled with frustration, that his grace is offered while his eyes are rolled. But that's what unconditional love is.

And unconditional love is what God chooses: unending love for imperfect people. I'm thankful. You should be too. Unconditional love is what God births in us. I'm a slow learner, but I'm seeing through my frustration in me to the source of grace, which is Jesus himself, and I'm seeing through my impatience with me to the goal, which is my growth. I'm not always there, but it's where I am today, and I'm praying this lesson sticks. If it did, it would mean a bit less of the mess that God has to clean up.

I am Bilbo. So is the church. The church is a stubborn, ugly pug with a propensity to mess on Jesus's sandals. And Jesus is the one on his knees, hugging it, washing its feet, saying, "We're going to fix you up, buddy."

God still loves it.

Stop going to church. Start being the church; be family. And together, let's walk toward *life*. Together, let's embrace the holiness Jesus has for us on the other side of religion. Joyfully, let's stand side by side, knee-deep in his grace.

There is incredible loveliness and victory to be found in the church, all over this nation and all over the world. There is noble sacrifice and radical generosity. There are sincere people struggling toward pure hearts and holy living. Ethnic groups and former enemies are being reconciled. There is also a good deal of mess, because the church is full of messy, broken people. But that's not the headline in this fallen world; that's just the setting. The real story is that Jesus loves her, anyway.

The vision God is leading my church, Overlake, toward is a big one. He is calling us to tackle some global giants through vibrant partnerships: to plant a thousand churches, to set a thousand sex slaves free, to see two thousand orphans who are currently on the streets be safely adopted into loving homes, and to establish fifty walk-in wellness centers combating HIV/AIDS. This beautiful vision will take all of God's people at Overlake working together for his glory, showing up in unlimited obedience, and trusting his incredible grace.

God's call on my life is only a little bit about me. It's mostly about his plan of tangibly showing his love on this broken planet. God's call often leads to greater calling. What I love is that it seems churches in the Northwest are bonding together, working together, and intentionally pursuing God's glory together. We are no longer the least churched region in America. Sparks of revival are beginning to smolder through the damp forest canopy of God's well-watered backyard that is our home.

But we can never get over his love for each one of us, imperfect as we are. Individually. Specifically. Carefully. He's gonna fix us up.

Because God's ultimate desire is grace.

MINING THE MESS: **MAKING IT PERSONAL**

Do you have a purpose statement for your life? Can you describe in, say, three to eight words the overarching goal that you live for? Can you summarize the things you are purposely living for and put it on the front of a T-shirt? Will people remember it? Does it make sense? Can a first grader "get" it?

I encourage you to think about the following purpose statements and work to craft your own:

> Jesus—seeking and saving the lost
> Paul—preaching the Good News to the Gentiles
> God—adopting a people through grace

What's your purpose?

I highly recommend placing your purpose statement on the same document that you produced when you were actively listening to God's call for your life. My prayer is that not only will you find that your purpose complements your call, you'll find that it helps you conceptualize all of the goals you sense God prompting you to pursue.

20

Glorious

G od says, "My thoughts are not your thoughts, and my ways are not your ways" (Isa. 55:8 GW). God will see more than you. God will see farther than you. God will see deeper than you. God will take the thing that looks like the end of the world and reveal it to be new life, a fresh start. He did it with the crucifixion, revealing the glory of the resurrection. Not a single disciple would have recommended that course of action. But that's because our ways are not God's ways nor are our thoughts his thoughts. That's also why it's important to seek a larger view.

The challenge is to move your perspective to God's perspective. Jonah certainly needed a paradigm shift:

> And the LORD said, "You pity the plant, for which you did not labor, nor did you make it grow, which came into being in a night and perished in a night. And should I not pity Nineveh, that great city, in which there are more than 120,000 persons who do not know their right hand from their left, and also much cattle?" (Jon. 4:10–11 ESV)

God essentially says, "You don't have my perspective. Grace is my perspective. One hundred twenty thousand lives are now being lived with purpose, transformed for eternity. People are beautiful to me. Nineveh is a great city that needed to reveal my glory. See the world the way I see the world." God cares about the economy of the city (i.e., cattle), and he cares about the well-being of the city (i.e., they don't know their right from their left). God calls the city "great" three times in the short book of Jonah. This simultaneously refers to its size and the fact that God thinks it's incredible. Why would God think a huge city filled with relatively ignorant, cattle-owning Ninevites is incredible? Because those are all people he loves. Nothing in all of creation is as amazing as a whole messy heap of image-bearers of the Almighty! That's God's perspective. He has compassion.

Shades of Clarity

We need to see the world through God's lens, which means we need a different pair of glasses.

I need sunglasses. I never have any around. Seattle has the highest consumption rate of sunglasses in America, by the way. When *el sol* comes out, it shocks us, and we're blinded. We can't see, we can't drive, and we can't find our caramel macchiatos, our fleece jackets, or the Birkenstocks we wear with REI wool socks. We rush to buy a new pair of sunglasses because we are moles. The sun then goes away (for a week, a month, six months), and we lose our sunglasses, recycle them into flowerpots, or compost them. Then one day, boom, the sun comes out, just like we didn't expect it to. We can't see anything, we buy another pair, and the cycle continues. But sunglasses paint the world a different shade. They alter your perspective.

Some of us in church world are wearing Coke-bottle glasses, big thick lenses that make our eyes look like we're in VeggieTales. We have an inappropriate focus on one theological position when we're wearing these. I love the recommendation form for applicants to Biola University (I've filled out hundreds of these over the years), which asks the question, "Does the applicant have any doctrinal views that are overemphasized?" Isn't that brilliant? Does this student only want to talk about Calvinism? Eschatology? Holy Spirit language? Politics? None of these things are problematic in themselves, but is the student well focused on *Jesus*? It's a good question. The best of us can get focused on secondary issues (like how I never wear shoes at football games because it's holy ground).

I know some folks in church world who wear the theological welder helmet. Their thinking goes like this: Everything is really dark and scary and hurtful, so I'll just protect myself and my family. We'll dig our freshwater well, make dresses out of drapes, marry our cousins, and sing "Kumbaya" until Jesus picks us up. We won't be the light of the world, but we will shout at the darkness. And we'll try not to see too much.

God Goggles

But we are called to put on God's glasses and see the world through the lens of his compassion, his grace. Jesus came to seek and save the lost. For God so loved the world. These things are central to the core reality of knowing and following Jesus. How do you get God's glasses? You simply get to know him. Spend time with him; spend time in his Word.

When you really begin to hear the heart of God, he says, "I'm not overly concerned about my reputation. I'm not concerned about how it looks in the tabloids. I created those people there. I love them. I want them to turn to me because I want them to be with me. I despise sin but I am in love with people, and I don't care how many times I have to shock a disgruntled prophet in my pursuit of souls!"

As Frederick Buechner put it in *The Hungering Dark*,

> Once they have seen him in a stable, they can never be sure where he will appear or to what lengths he will go or to what ludicrous depths of self-humiliation he will descend in his wild pursuit of man. If holiness and the awful power of God were present in this least auspicious of all events, this birth of a peasant's child, then there is no place or time so lowly and earthbound but that holiness can be present there too. And this means that we are never safe, that there is no place where we can hide from God, no place where we are safe from his power to break in two and recreate the human heart because it is just where he seems most helpless that he is most strong, and just where we least expect him that he comes most fully.[9]

This is God pursuing a fallen humanity. There are no depths to which he will not descend. The king of the universe was born in a barn! The king of glory chose abject humility. The hands that shaped the mountains were pierced by spikes that held him in torture until he gave up his spirit. The motive for these painfully humiliating situations was nothing more than love. For love, obedience, and the glory of the Father. For love, grace, and the pursuit of you. Trying to write off God's love will always be a frustrating endeavor.

Think for a moment about the *irony*. The only one who legitimately deserves absolute obedience and praise, the only one who is worthy of a trembling respect at all times from all of humanity, the only one who really has a right to concern over his reputation because his reputation is impeccable, the only one who has that right to demand unconditional regard for his reputation—he actually trusts his reputation to a bunch of yahoos like us.

So we are Christ's ambassadors; God is making his appeal through us. We speak for Christ when we plead, "Come back to God!" (2 Cor. 5:20)

He says, "You be my ambassadors. I don't care about my reputation; I only care about love. Now you do the same. Don't be concerned about your reputation. Be concerned only about my love. Plead with the great city to come back to me." Jesus bleeds grace. These are the goggles God wears.

His perspective is love.

The End . . . or the Beginning

The great thing about the book of Jonah is that it just ends. Finis. No resolution. Totally open-ended, like a French film with subtitles that won some awards but died at the box office. "You mean that's *it?*"

Does Jonah get it? Does he lighten up and laugh at himself and say, "*Holy mackerel!*" (pun intended—well, not at first, but then I got it)? "God, you're right! I started this thing selfishly with my own agenda, and I'm finishing selfishly with my own agenda. I've had it all wrong! It is all about you! You called me into this thing; you found me playing hide-and-seek; you saved me. Then you used my obedience to introduce your compassion to Nineveh. I get it! I get it! Thanks for being patient with me, but I get it now!" Goofy sigh, followed by Brady Bunch laughter. The end. Play Randy Newman song. Roll credits. Cue bloopers.

We don't really know how the story ends. The Bible does not include *Jonah Part 2: The Tarshish Chronicles.* This is as it should be. You see, Jonah's fish story isn't really about Jonah at all. The book of Jonah is a snapshot of God's heart. God, Creator and Lord, says, "I love you all! Everyone! Israelites and Ninevites! Muslims and Jews and Hindus and Moonies and Baptists and Catholics and all of those who profess to hold to no 'ism' at all! I love Republicans and Democrats! I love Nineveh, and that's why I sent Jonah . . . I love the *world*, and that's why I sent *Jesus*!"

Because of Jonah, we see the unconditional, unending, unyielding, unfailing love of God for imperfect people.

That is why Jesus says, in Matthew 12, "You want a sign? I'll give you a sign: Jonah. Three days in the belly of a whale to emerge proclaiming love for a wayward nation . . . and I will spend three days in the belly of the earth to emerge proclaiming God's love for a wayward planet." No matter where you are or what you are going through, God's love is real and proven for you. God sent Jonah to save Nineveh as a precursor to God sending Jesus to save the world.

The book ends without a resolution in Jonah's life, but I like to believe he finally got it. In fact, I think we can safely conclude he finally understood God's heart. Tim Keller opened up this truth for me in a sermon. Here's the reasoning: Who wrote the book of Jonah? How do we know of an idiot prophet who ran from Yahweh until God put him in a fish? How do we know the story of a guy who was barely, momentarily obedient, saved one hundred twenty thousand souls, and then immediately had a poutfest about it? Jonah himself tells us. This is his journal. And only a person humbled and amazed at God's relentless love, only a person at the very end of his reputation and privilege and judgment would reveal to the ages what an absolute mess he consistently was but how God's glory shone ever brighter in the midst of it.

I believe Jonah gets it. But the more important question is: Do we? Are we in? Are you developing a heart for those who don't know about God's grace? Are you ready to build the foundation of your life upon a clear call to help others understand that the God of the universe is crazy about them?

> The fruit of the righteous is a tree of life,
> and he who wins souls is wise. (Prov. 11:30 NKJV)

This is the wisdom to which God calls each and every one of us. Look back to the first verse in the book of Jonah:

> The word of the LORD came to Jonah son of Amittai. (Jon. 1:1 NIV)

The word of the Lord came to . . . Mike. The word of the Lord came to . . . Jodie. The word of the Lord came to . . . Chad. The word of the Lord came to . . . (insert your name here). Do you run? Or do you respond?

Maybe you're here, all the way through this book about a prophet named Jonah, and you have never called out to God. You've been tracking through each stage of Jonah's run and God's love. You've heard about God's call on your life. You've seen that when you run from God, you end up in a glorious mess, and you've understood that when you obey God, you see incredible things happen. What you need to do right now, without another moment passing, is simply call out to God. He loves you so much. When you cry out to God, you'll discover, like so many others have, that those who trust *him* are not disappointed.

> They cried to you and were saved.
> They trusted you and were never disappointed. (Ps. 22:5 GW)

Or perhaps you've called and been helped. You've been rescued. You've trusted God and have not been disappointed. What is it going to take for you to offer that same kind of love to others? We don't know if Jonah ever loves the Nineveh he was sent to save. But we do know Jesus loves the world he was sent to save.

Are you in? Are you ready to embrace God's amazing, sanctifying grace? The first words of the story of Jonah are God's words. The last words of the story of Jonah are God's as well. May I suggest to you that God gets the first and last word in your story too. And in mine. It's God's story, after all.

And we are invited into it.

Father Love

This brings me to the close of this glorious mess, at least for now.

One day several years ago, when we still lived in California and I was still driving my old '79 Suburban, I was leaving my home and heading to church when God gave me a moment that burned itself into my mind. It just so happened that my wife was on the front porch, holding my infant son and waving good-bye to Daddy with my daughter, Alex, who was three. It was a *Leave It to Beaver* moment, and not all that typical. I pulled my roaring, nonenvironmentally friendly Suburban out of the driveway, waved to my family, and began to drive away. I noticed that my daughter was shouting something to me. She was shouting so hard that each word bounced her up on the tiptoes of her cute bare feet, and she really wanted me to hear her, but I couldn't hear her because I was driving a '79 Suburban. So I pulled back over to the curb, rolled down the window, and as I cut the engine, I heard the words, "Don't forget! Don't forget, okay? Don't forget . . . (deep breath) . . . I LOVE YOU!"

It killed me. In a moment of supernatural import, I sensed God was speaking to me those same words: *Don't forget, Mike. Don't forget, okay? Don't forget . . . I LOVE YOU!*

There was holiness all over those words. Because I know me. I don't look lovely. I don't feel lovable. So much of the time, I don't act loveworthy. The word I've used to describe me is *mess.* And yet, there it is. God doesn't pretend I'm lovely. God doesn't lie and say I'm lovable when he knows I'm not. No, but because of Jesus Christ, *I am lovely.* He is the beloved Son, and in him, I'm beloved as well. He chooses to love me, just as I am. His glory shows up in me and through me. It really is a miraculous, confusing, glorious mess. This is my deepest reality, and this is true for all who are in Christ as well.

In the midst of your journey, in the midst of your call and your response, my prayer is that you'll be still enough to feel the touch of God and quiet enough to hear the whisper of his delight over you. He loves you. *Don't forget! Don't forget! Don't forget . . . I love you!* Do you understand these are his words over you? This is his heart over you. You are a mess. You are. But he has made you lovely, lovable, and loveworthy.

You are lovely in how he made you. You are lovely in how he saved you. You are lovely in how he fills you. You are lovely in what he calls you to. All of this is how his glory shines out on this fallen heartbreak, illuminating hope like the world's first dawn.

And he is calling you into the fullness of his life and his grace so that you can extend that same life and grace to others. Don't run from him. Tell him yes. Experience his grace. Be ready to share it. And prepare for the ride of your life. I promise you this:

It'll be a glorious mess.

But mostly glorious.

Epilogue

God is a Father. Our Father.

And his love for you is indescribable. Not later, when you've cleaned yourself up. Not when you've got it all together. Not when you know all the right answers. Not when you've got time. You. Now. As you are. Are loved. Completely. And the same is true about what you can accomplish. Significant. Life changing. Eternal. Legacy. You. Now. As you are. God is calling you. Realize that you live and move and breathe under his amazing grace. In grace he saves you from sin. In grace he saves you for life. You'll never get beyond it. Don't try. Just receive it, and offer it to others.

Tonight I took a run in the twilight. I was running only a few miles tonight, just a warm down from yesterday's eighteen-miler, and it was gorgeous.

Bats were flitting around the cool evening. I startled a coyote in the distance. The silhouettes of pine needles and maple leaves were so sharp in the deepening translucence you could cut yourself on them. I was loving Jesus as I ran, thankful for this long day, thankful for the soccer games and the sunshine, thankful for friends and family, thankful for church.

Then the music on my playlist changed to a song by Sigur Rós called "Glósóli." This is a band from Iceland, and they don't sing in English but in some hauntingly mythic language (probably whatever Björk giggles in). The song begins like a whisper and then builds like

183

a hurricane, but the whole thing is so beautiful it resonates deeply on an emotional level. The video that goes with the song is more of a short film, really (well worth a trip to YouTube). As I ran, I played it in my mind.

There is a boy with a drum. He begins to journey. As he travels, he enlists other children to join him on his journey. Each beautiful child is symbolic; they are metaphors for the innocence, the magnificence, and the brokenness of humanity. Two of them are frightened, and so they've hidden behind masks. Another pair have learned violence somehow. This one is isolated, alone. This one knows love. The boy with the drum calls them, and they all come. They leave whatever life they have known; they drop their nets, as it were, and they join this quest, this parade, this journey. When the boy with the drum arrives at the place he has been leading them to, he looks deliberately at the horizon. He sets his face toward Jerusalem, if you will. And then he beats his drum.

He beats his drum.

He beats his drum.

With wild abandon, he begins to run with all he has forward, upward, over a gently sloping, grass-covered hillside. The other children join him. It is serious, ecstatic, jubilant, triumphant. The drum is cast aside. The final masks are removed. The children run upward and upward until they reach the very edge of an impossibly high cliff.

And then they soar off the edge.

They soar.

Faces beaming, they soar.

And that's the end. We don't know the backstory; we don't know the future story. Here they are. They find one another. They journey together. They run. They soar. All led by a boy with a drum. It is epic, adventurous, glorious. And it's for us as well.

The call of Jesus leads us to life.

He didn't just come to set us free—he came to set us free indeed. He will lead you where he is calling you. And I believe even now he's beating his drum, willing to show you what it takes to soar if you'll follow him.

Run with him.

Soar.

It was dark as I finished my run. The song was over, and there was a lump in my throat. I walked the last bit in silence, listening to the sounds of the night. I felt joyful, quiet, serious. It is a good thing to know the drummer. It is a good thing to follow him to the heights.

Small Group Discussion Guide

Some things are truly frightening, like realizing you've had a piece of lettuce stuck in your tooth the entire day, even during that conversation with your potential love interest. Some things are sheer joy, like realizing as you wake up in the morning that school is out and the holidays have begun. Small groups can be a bit of both: some terror, some bliss. This Small Group Discussion Guide is written in the hope that the bliss far outweighs the terror as you work through *Glorious Mess*.

How to Make the Most of It

The first step is joining a small group. Get involved with a small group at the church you're plugged into, or simply grab a few friends and form your own group for reading through this book together. There are only five weeks, corresponding to the five sections of *Glorious Mess*, so make the decision to get the most out of it by being committed. By committing time to reading and to your group, you provide an opportunity for trust and friendship to grow.

Speak up in your small group. Your opinion is valuable. Someone else is probably thinking things through in a similar fashion and could learn from your experience. If you don't share, a valuable opportunity for others to learn will be lost.

Conversely, be a listener. Every person has value, and we are all at a unique place in our faith journey. This doesn't mean you need to agree with everyone's opinion, but everyone needs to be valued.

This guide is loosely based upon the five sections of *Glorious Mess*, and each week's guide contains three parts: a verse to *read*, some questions to *respond* to, and a challenge or prayer to *reflect* upon. Approach each lesson with an open heart to the things God might teach you in dialogue with others along the journey. Each small group session is followed up by two sections written for you to do on your own. They are called "Looking into Yourself" and "Looking into the Word." These are to help you take a deeper look inside yourself and into the Scriptures.

Faith Is a Daily Decision

The most important thing for anyone who wants to follow Jesus to remember is this: faith is a daily decision. Filling in the blanks or knowing all the answers won't necessarily grow your faith. But allowing yourself to be real, and then taking what you've learned and putting it into practice, will change your life and probably the lives of those around you. Thanks for taking a risk. I pray that this experience helps. I hope you have fun and in the process become more of the person God has created you to be!

Week 1: Listening to God's Voice

Read

For nothing is impossible with God. (Luke 1:37 NLT)

The word of the LORD came to Jonah son of Amittai: "Go to the great city of Nineveh and preach against it, because its wickedness has come up before me." (Jon. 1:1–2 NIV)

Respond

1. How familiar are you with the book of Jonah? What were your previous impressions?
2. Is it difficult to believe that this story actually took place? Why or why not?
3. Do you believe that nothing is impossible with God? Point to one example in your own life.
4. We looked at a few examples of men and women who had been called by God. What was going through your mind when we looked at God's call for them? How were their calls similar? How were they different?
5. How do you think God is calling you? Have you audibly heard his voice? If not, then what are some other ways that God calls us?

6. The great commandment (love God and love people; see Luke 10:27) is for all believers. How does this general call cover all others?
7. How will God's call require you to take a step of faith? Have you ever experienced this? What happened when you stepped out in faith? How did you grow?

Reflect

God is calling you to something great, and what he calls you to, he will empower you for. Nothing is impossible with him. Close by praying for one another. Pray that God clarifies a glorious obsession that you can pursue with joy. Pray that God gives you the faith to pursue it with expectancy!

Looking into Yourself

1. Who are those people who give you wise counsel?
2. Have you ever gone against the advice of trusted friends? What happened?
3. Have you ever withheld information from trusted friends because you didn't want their advice? What happened then?
4. Write down three reasons that it is important to humbly listen to the advice of trusted counsel.
5. What are your goals?
6. What are you passionate about?
7. Are you challenging yourself right now?
8. Are you making a contribution?
9. How does it make you feel to know that the power that raised Jesus from the dead is available to you? If you really believed that for one day, how would that day look? What would be different about your actions? about your conversations? about your daydreams?
10. Why is humility an important attitude to have when listening to God?
11. What does God's character have to do with God's call on our lives?
12. What is God calling you to do with your life? What is God calling you to do this year? How about this week? How about right now?

Looking into the Word

Take a look at the following responses to God's call:

1. *Jeremiah 1:4–9*. Imagine this scene as if God were speaking directly to you. What fears would he be calming for you? Write out your own response to God's call.
2. *Luke 1:38*. How did Mary respond to God's call? What was the result of her obedience?
3. *Matthew 26:42*. How did Jesus model obedience for us? Can you pray the same prayer that he prayed?
4. The following verses all have something to say about clarifying God's call on our lives. Write in your own words the lessons found in each one.

James 1:13

James 2:15–16

Matthew 17:20

Proverbs 15:22

Psalms 37:4

James 4:7, 10

1 John 3:22–23

Week 2: Running from God

Read

But Jonah ran away from the LORD and headed for Tarshish. He went down to Joppa, where he found a ship bound for that port. After paying the fare, he went aboard and sailed for Tarshish to flee from the LORD. (Jon. 1:3 NIV)

> Where can I go from your Spirit?
>   Where can I flee from your presence?
> If I go up to the heavens, you are there;
>   if I make my bed in the depths, you are there. (Ps. 139:7–8 NIV)

Respond

1. When Jonah ran from the Lord, he fell asleep—he tuned out spiritually. What are some ways that people "tune out" or "fall asleep" spiritually?
2. What are some things that you have done to tune out in the past?
3. Are you still doing those things?
4. What does God's omniscience mean for your life?
5. What does his omnipotence mean for your life?
6. How about his omnipresence?
7. What does it mean to be convicted by the Holy Spirit?

8. Have you ever experienced his conviction? How did you experience it?
9. What was going on in your life? How did you respond to that conviction?

Reflect

How ironic it is that there are areas of our lives where we are trying to run from God—when what he wants for us is our best! Think about God's best for your life:

- What does it look like?
- What does it feel like?
- What is it going to take for you to embrace it?
- What are you waiting for?

Looking into Yourself

1. Is it encouraging to think that we can't outrun God? Is it depressing? What are some motivations that people have for hiding from God?
2. When our relationship with God is out of alignment, we see the results in all of our other relationships and activities. Have you found this to be true?
3. Have you also found that there are seasons when it is possible to fake it? How does it feel to be in the middle of a season where you are pretending?
4. What does it take to get right with God? What is difficult about this? What attitudes do we need to overcome?
5. When Jonah was thrown overboard, people ended up praising God. What had they experienced? How are nonbelievers moved to praise God?
6. How can your life encourage others to praise God?
7. What are ten words that come to mind when you think about God's love?
8. How do you interact with God's love on a daily basis?

Looking into the Word

1. Read about God's call to Isaiah in Isaiah 6:1–8.

2. Now read Jonah 1:1–17.
3. What strikes you about the difference between these two situations? Write in your own words the lessons that come from each situation.
4. Identify your response within these two stories. Which one comes nearer to yours?
5. What does God want you to know?
6. What attitude does God want you to show?
7. Where does God want to get your attention?

Week 3: Getting Out of Your Glorious Mess

Read

> When my life was ebbing away,
>   I remembered you, LORD,
> and my prayer rose to you,
>   to your holy temple.
> Those who cling to worthless idols
>   turn away from God's love for them.
> But I, with shouts of grateful praise,
>   will sacrifice to you.
> What I have vowed I will make good.
> I will say, "Salvation comes from the LORD." (Jon. 2:7–9
> NIV)

Respond

1. Have you ever been in a totally stuck place?
2. What is the worst mess that your choices have ever put you in? (Or the worst mess you feel comfortable sharing?) How did you feel?
3. What was the precise moment that you realized you really were in trouble?
4. What is the healthiest response to finding yourself in a messy situation?

5. Most of humanity knows deep down that pursuing the world's way leads to pain. Spend a moment reaffirming that truth in your group. How have you seen this in your own life?
6. Why is Jonah a great example for us in this area?
7. What are some things that strike you about his prayer in Jonah 2:7–9?
8. How do those who cling to idols miss out on God's love?
9. Look at verse 9. How is Jonah able to claim that salvation comes from the Lord? What does Jonah model for us here?

Reflect

Pray together to close your small group time:

"Lord Jesus Christ, thank you that on the cross, you paid the price for my glorious mess. Because of the work you did on the cross, I'm unstuck, I'm set free, and I'm thankful. Salvation comes only from you, and, Lord, you set me free for a purpose! Allow me to live free this week and fulfill my purpose!"

Looking into Yourself

1. Do you believe that God gives us what we need most? Why or why not?
2. Because the Lord gave a ram to Abraham to sacrifice on the mountain, Abraham names the place Yahweh-yireh, which means "The LORD will provide" (see Gen. 22:14). Write down some ways that God has provided for you. Then spend some time being thankful for his provision.
3. Have you been running from God in any part of your life? Where? Why? Where has it led you?
4. Are you ready to come back, to come clean, to give it all, to surrender the fight to a God who wants your best?
5. Read Proverbs 2:3–5. Are you ready to pursue wisdom with this intensity?
6. Is it difficult for you to trust God? Why or why not?
7. One of the tragedies of the temptation of Adam and Eve is that Satan planted a lie in the human heart that has lived there ever since. It's the lie that "God isn't good. If he was good, he wouldn't deny you that forbidden fruit." Do you think that lie is affecting your faith today? How?
8. What are some constant areas of doubt for you?

9. Do you trust that God works for your best?
10. Are you experiencing the joy of his salvation?
11. What will it take for you to walk in joy with him?

Looking into the Word

1. Read 1 Samuel 3:10–11 and Psalm 9:10. Together, these verses describe the attitude that we seek to have when God calls.
2. Repentance is an essential concept when we think about getting out of our glorious mess. What does repentance mean to you?
3. What does it mean to God?
4. Read Acts 2:38–42. There are many aspects of the repentance found in this passage. List some of the implications. How did repentance change the lives of the believers? Has it changed your life in a similar manner?
5. What areas of your life still need to be submitted to God's love?
6. What does it mean to be a saint?
7. What does it meant to be one of God's kids? Does it mean that you'll live a perfect life? Why or why not?

Week 4: Seeing God Work

Read

Then the word of the LORD came to Jonah a second time: "Go to the great city of Nineveh and proclaim to it the message I give you." Jonah obeyed the word of the LORD and went to Nineveh. Now Nineveh was a very large city; it took three days to go through it. (Jon. 3:1–3 NIV)

Respond

1. What is one area in your life where you have experienced God giving you a second chance?
2. What is one area where you've seen him give you second chance after second chance?
3. Is this an area you're still struggling with? How can this small group support you in the midst of it?
4. Do you believe that God is the one who does the work of changing hearts? Why or why not? What else might be necessary?
5. If God alone can change hearts, then why did Jonah need to go to Nineveh at all? Could God have done it without Jonah?
6. Why did God want to partner with Jonah in this work?
7. Why does he want to partner with you?
8. Are you committed to absolute obedience? If not, what is holding you back?

9. If so, have you invited safe friends to challenge you? Are you allowing your small group to hold you accountable in this kind of radical obedience?
10. What God did through Jonah was incredible, and it's nothing compared to what God can do through your obedience. Read that statement again. Do you believe it?
11. Are you ready to do whatever God calls you to do?

Reflect

God has good things in store for you. God will be with you to accomplish more than you could ever dream on your own. Jump in! Hold your plans with an open palm, and watch God magnify them.

Looking into Yourself

1. Why is our attitude important as we move to obey God?
2. What does our attitude communicate to the world?
3. Give yourself an attitude checkup:
   - Where is my attitude toward obeying God?
   - Why do I feel that way?
   - Have I thanked God for saving me today?
   - Have I thanked God for blessing me richly?
   - Have I taken an inventory of his blessings lately?
4. Do I have a vision for where God is moving me?
5. When I look back at my life, can I identify where growth has taken place?
6. Have I praised God for that growth today?

Looking into the Word

1. Read Judges 6:12–7:22. It's a long passage, but it's worth it. This is the story of Gideon and how God used his faithfulness to win an overwhelming victory against all odds.
2. Spend a few moments writing down every truth that you can apply to your life from this passage.
3. Spend a few moments being thankful that God is able to do amazing things through your faithfulness and obedience.

Week 5: Embracing God's Amazing Grace

Read

So he prayed to the LORD, "LORD, isn't this what I said would happen when I was still in my own country? That's why I tried to run to Tarshish in the first place. I knew that you are a merciful and compassionate God, patient, and always ready to forgive and to reconsider your threats of destruction. So now, LORD, take my life. I'd rather be dead than alive." The LORD asked, "What right do you have to be angry?" (Jon. 4:2–4 GW)

Respond

1. Describe why Jonah became angry. What was he concerned about? Were his concerns legitimate?
2. How did God view his concerns?
3. What do you want the foundation of your life built upon?
4. Are you a "people pleaser"?
5. Do you change who you are depending upon what social circle you are in? Are you different at work, at home, at school, in social settings?
6. Are there times when those fluctuations are appropriate? How do you know?
7. Paul says that he strives to become all things to all people so that he might win some. Is that a priority in your life?
8. What are some healthy priorities that cause people to morph their personality to match their surroundings?

9. At the end of the book, it is a bit incredible that Jonah is still caught up in judgment. But many believers are still focused on God's judgment. Are you?

10. What are the issues in your life where it is easier to respond with judgment than grace?

11. What are you going to do about those things?

12. Do you believe there is no condemnation for those who are in Christ? If that's what God offers you, doesn't it make sense that we would offer that grace to others?

Reflect

The main lesson of the book of Jonah is one of mercy. God walks through a process of mercy with his reluctant prophet. Then God demonstrates mercy to a repentant people. Finally, God ends up describing his mercy to his mercy-receiving but not mercy-giving prophet. Commit to being on board with God's mercy. Commit to becoming God's agent of grace!

Looking into Yourself

1. Describe in your own words the lesson of the vine (or the lesson of the worm). What was God trying to show Jonah? What is God trying to teach you?

2. Why do you think God isn't all that concerned about his "reputation"?

3. Read Philippians 2:5–11. This passage says ultimately all will bow before the awesome glory of God. What does this verse say about God's "reputation"?

4. We don't know ultimately how Jonah responded to God's incredible grace. We can guess, because he's probably the one who rats himself out. But you are the only one who determines how you respond to it. Are you in? Do you get it? How have you responded to God's grace? How are you responding to his call to share grace with a world that starves for it?

5. What do you need to do to ensure that your "reputation" won't prevent you from responding?

Looking into the Word

1. Read Matthew 18:21–35. Some incredible lessons of forgiveness are contained within this passage.
2. What does this passage say about God's heart?
3. What does it say about God's will for us?
4. Spend time each day this week reading this passage. Each time you read it, ask God to show you a situation in your life where you need to offer forgiveness.

May God bless you as you model and distribute his grace!

Many Thanks

Like many authors before me, I recognize that on my own, this work would not have been brought to completion. I'd love to share my love and gratitude.

Thanks to the elders, staff, and good people of Overlake Christian Church, who have been an honor and a joy to journey with. You are truly beautiful! Thanks to Marc Bauman (the kind of elder chair that every single one of my pastor friends prays for), Dana Erickson (who gambled on me and won, or lost, depending on how he looks at things), Rick Kingham (for loving me even as we went through the bowel of the beast together), Rick Warren (who showed me a truly glorious ministry model), and my parents, Lonnie and Nancy Howerton, who instilled within me the twin mantras of confident living (Rule #1: Believe in yourself! Rule #2: Keep your eye on the ball!).

Thanks to those who played a more direct hand in this project, without whose gentle and expert touch this book would lack any discernible marks of quality. Thanks to Jeff Locke at Docent Research, who kept me theologically sound. Thanks to Doug Fields, who is a friend and mentor to me in style of communication (self-deprecating), style of ministry (relational), and strength of character (humble and wise, both of which I'm still working on). Thanks to Leigh Sarti, who prompted me to begin writing in the first place years ago, and to Greg Swineheart for his humor and for seeing the need and offering help freely. Thanks to Gary Gonzalez, Josh and Neely McQueen, and Scott Lee for edits and encouragement, and thanks to Chad Allen and the others at Baker for taking a risk on an unknown author and for clear, succinct, polite suggestions.

Heartfelt thanks to my wife, Jodie, and to my kids, Alexandra, Caleb, and Duzi, for being without doubt the most glorious parts of my glorious mess.

Most of all, I want to thank you, Jesus, for refusing to give up on me. I will never recover from the awesome truth that your grace is sufficient for me.

Notes

1. Henri Nouwen, *Making All Things New* (New York: HarperCollins, 1981), 46–47, emphasis added.

2. Frederick Buechner, *Wishful Thinking: A Theological ABC* (New York: Harper & Row, 1973), 95.

3. I first heard a version of this story from Rick Warren, but for details on Dantzig's life, see http://en.wikipedia.org/wiki/George_Dantzig and http://www.snopes.com/college/homework/unsolvable.asp.

4. A. W. Tozer, *The Price of Neglect* (Camp Hill, PA: Christian Publications, 1991), 12.

5. A summary of Lincoln's failures and successes can be found at Abraham Lincoln Online, "Lincoln's 'Failures'?" 2010, http://showcase.netins.net/web/creative/lincoln/education/failures.htm.

6. "Lufkin, Texas, Concert Transcript: Carpenter's Way Christian Church, July 19, 1997," Calling Out Your Name, http://www.kidbrothers.net/words/concert-transcripts/lufkin-texas-jul1997-full.html.

7. Justin Taylor, "How Much Do You Have to Hate Someone to *Not* Proselytize?" *Between Two Worlds* (blog), The Gospel Coalition website, November 17, 2009, http://thegospelcoalition.org/blogs/justintaylor/2009/11/17/how-much-do-you-have-to-hate-somebody-to-not-proselytize/.

8. Rick Warren, October 15, 2010, https://twitter.com/#!/RickWarren/status/27447472881.

9. Frederick Buechner, *The Hungering Dark* (New York: HarperCollins, 1969), 13–14.

Mike Howerton is lead pastor of Overlake Christian Church in Redmond, Washington, and served for six years as the college pastor at Saddleback Church. He is a graduate of Pepperdine University and received his master's degree from Fuller Theological Seminary. Mike lives on the east side of Seattle with his wife, Jodie; their three children, Alex, Caleb, and Duzi; and a couple of surfboards that aren't used nearly enough.

Check Out GloriousMess.org!

To learn how you can introduce your church to *Glorious Mess*, please visit GloriousMess.org where you'll find more resources from Mike Howerton including:

- **sermon outlines**
- **teaching videos**
- **small group curriculum**

To connect with others also participating in the "Glorious Mess" journey, please visit us on Facebook at facebook.com/gloriousmess